The Preservation of Wildlife in India

The Preservation of Wildlife in India

Reprinted from the Journal of
The Bombay Natural History Society

BIOTECH

2008

Biotech Books

Delhi - 110 035

Originally Published 1934–1936
First Indian Impression 1988
Second Indian Impression 2008

ISBN10 81-7622-193-7
ISBN13 978-81-7622-193-1

Published by : **BIOTECH BOOKS**
1123/74, Tri Nagar,
DELHI – 110 035
Phone: 27383999
e-mail: biotechbooks@yahoo.co.in

Showroom : 4762-63/23, Ansari Road, Darya Ganj,
NEW DELHI - 110 002
Phone: 23245578, 23244987

Printed at : **Chawla Offset Printers**
New Delhi – 110 052

PRINTED IN INDIA

The Preservation of Wild Life in India.

THE PRESERVATION OF WILD LIFE IN INDIA.

No. 1. *THE CENTRAL PROVINCES.*

BY

A. A. DUNBAR-BRANDER.

(Late Conservator of Forests, Central Provinces.)

Game Country: Status and Jurisdiction.

Good game tracts exist both in Indian State and in British India.

The British Government has no jurisdiction over the game in Indian States. Most of the Indian Princes protect game, and there is a growing tendency for this movement to spread and become more vigorous. In most States the laws or rules for the protection of wild animals are effectively enforced.

No more need be said about the States. With regard to British India, game is found in country having a different legal status, and this must be differentiated:—

(*a*) Private land.
(*b*) State land.

Generally speaking, game in (*a*) has no owner. It belongs neither to the owner of the land nor to the State. The Government, however, has the right to pass laws regulating the slaughter of game, and in most cases such laws have been passed. I shall refer to this in more detail when dealing with game laws.

With regard to State land the great bulk of which consists of Government forest, the State owns the game, and special laws dealing with its protection throughout India have been passed. These laws are administered by the Forest Department. I shall also refer to this in some detail later on.

Types of Game Country.

There are four main types of country in which game is found and which I have designated as follows:—

(1) Himalayan.
(2) Terai.
(3) Central Plateau.
(4) Southern.

Position with regard to Protection in each Type.

Himalayan.—The terrain in which the game is found is its chief protection. To destroy it entails arduous and whole-time work, quite incompatible with any prospective profits to the poacher, and, save with regard to certain species which frequent the outer hills, no special measures are called for with regard to this tract.

The Terai.—Very much the same applies to the Terai, but for different causes. This tract of country extends from Dehra Dun along the Himalayan foothills eastward into Assam and thence southward towards the Bay of Bengal. In it the jungle and grasses are so dense that no serious slaughter of game can take place without the extensive use of elephants. These, of course, cannot be employed without sanction and regulation. The amount of game and species to be killed can, therefore, be regulated; game is holding its own and no special measures seem called for in this tract.

The Central Plateau.—This tract embraces the great mass of India and was at one time the finest shooting country and contained the finest fauna in the East. The forest is generally open and although often hilly the hills are no deterrent to a hunter. Unlike the other tracts, nature of the terrain in the Central Plateau is an inadequate protection. Further, the game-holding tracts are not only surrounded by a dense population, but a large interior population of aborigines exists inside the forest itself, to an extent not found in the other tracts. It is in this tract that the recent disappearance of game has been so lamentable and calls for the most urgent remedial measures.

I left India in 1922 but revisited it in 1928, and was appalled to find such a change in so short a period, quite common species being found only with difficulty. The finest game country in this tract is found in the Central Provinces, and I shall deal at some length with the causes which have brought about this state of affairs in that area, as I believe they have a very wide application.

The Southern Type.—As I do not know this country personally I write about it with some diffidence. I have, however, taken a very deep interest in all that pertains to game during my whole service in India, and I believe the following to be fundamentally true. The country is very mountainous and the cover is often dense: less mountainous, of course, than even the outer spurs of the Himalayas, and less dense than the Terai. Nevertheless the combination of these two factors in the same area makes the destruction of game by no means easy; and so far as I know the game is fairly well holding its own except in outlying portions.

Position of Game on Private Lands.

As already stated, the game in private lands has no owner. The State has passed laws prohibiting the killing of does and immature animals, sitting over water, and the use of various methods of destruction. To all intents and purposes the laws are a dead letter as there is no preventive staff. The two main preventive services in India are the Police and the Forest Service. The latter has no jurisdiction outside State forest, and the Police take no interest in enforcing the rules. Prosecutions are very rare, and any interest the local constable may take in the matter would often be to share in the booty. The result is that game has almost disappeared from private lands. The main Bombay-Allahabad line runs through some 200 miles of antelope country. Twenty years ago one was almost constantly in sight of herds. In 1928 in four hours I only saw two small herds, watching from the train. The only fauna left in private lands is a few chital and sambhar in specially favoured localities, pig in considerable numbers, and a sprinkling of antelope, also lesser carnivora.

The great mass of the country, however, is blank and it will be readily understood that these blank unprotected spaces surrounding Government forest which contain game act as a constant drain on the stock of fauna in the protected lands: there is constant leakage to destruction. In my opinion nothing can save the fauna in these private lands. Its extermination is certain. The people have been educated to destroy it: there is no staff to protect it, and even if the Indian Legislatures could be induced to take measures, financial considerations preclude adequate protection.

State Lands: Position of Game.

These mostly consist of State forests where the Forest Act and the rules made thereunder apply; amongst these are included the rules regulating the killing of game. On the whole, these are excellent, and, although I shall suggest certain stiffening to meet modern conditions, nevertheless it is not in the rules themselves but in their application that failure arises. As regards the European and Indian sportsmen who enter the forest to shoot under permit, the rules are absolutely efficacious, and this type of sportsman does no harm. Where they fail is in the prevention of poaching. There is lucrative trade in game; the initial detection of poaching often rests with a lowly-paid forest guard. Men possessing guns often command respect, and the guard finds the easiest plan is to take a percentage of the profits. Moreover, special rewards, which the rules sanction in poaching cases, are far too sparingly given, and the magistrates' sentences are often quite inadequate.

The Main Reasons why the Destruction of Game has Recently Increased.

(1) During the war the rules were relaxed. In certain cases the shooting of does was permitted to make leather jackets for sailors. There was a general activity in the trade in the products of game: tanneries came into being, and what was previously an occasional trade has now become an active competitive one with wide ramifications: a slaughtered deer no longer means merely a gorge of meat for the local aborigines, it is an article of commerce and a valuable one.

(2) There has been a very large increase in the number of gun licences issued as well as a large increase in unlicensed or illegal guns. It is easy to see that with a large number of guns legally possessed, the detection of illegal guns becomes more difficult.

Be the causes what they may, the State forests are surrounded by guns, many of which are constantly used in destroying game both inside the forest and just outside it. In the present political situation any attempt to regulate the number of guns to actual requirements for crop-protection is hopeless. The guns have come, and to stay.

(3) *The Motor Car.*—This is perhaps the biggest factor of all, in the disappearance of game, although without the two previous causes its significance would be small. Since the war whole tracts have been opened up—in fact no tract is inviolate—cars penetrating along dirt tracks into country in one day which previously took a week's marching with camels and horses. Every car that moves by day or night has one or more guns in it, and practically every animal seen which presents a fair chance of being killed, without further questions asked, is fired at. Moreover, expeditions go out at night with strong moveable searchlights and shoot down whatever is encountered, and the car enables the booty to be removed. The destruction is terrible. I came across glaring cases during my short three months' trip in 1928. The present game laws were framed before this menace arose, and they require to be reviewed and amended in consequence.

Some Remedial Measures Suggested.

(1) An attempt to check the increase of guns, even reduce them.

(2) Much stricter control and regulation of tanneries and businesses trading in wild fauna and its products.

(3) Complete review of the rules so as to deal with the motor car amongst other things, and to bring the owner and the driver of any car within the penalties of law-breaking.

(4) Press for stiffer sentences in poaching cases and rewards to subordinates detecting the same. These rewards are at present optional, but should be made as a matter of course, save for definite reasons.

(5) Establishing associations for the protection of Wild Life and housing enlightened Indian opinion, and enlisting influential men as members of such Societies.

Sanctuaries.

As will be seen from what I have written above, the Himalayan and Terai areas are hardly suitable places, even if required, in which to create National Sanctuaries. With regard to the Central and Southern areas, the case is different. In these tracts they will form a useful and interesting purpose, especially in the former, where the fauna can be readily observed, will readily tame, and be a delight to visitors.

My knowledge of the Southern tract does not enable me to suggest any particular area, but as I know every square mile of the Central Provinces I can definitely assert that one area is suited *par excellence* for a National Park. This is known as the Banjar Valley Reserve.

The Banjar Valley Reserve.

Situation.—Situated in the South Mandla Forest Division, 30 miles south-east of Mandla, which is the District Head-quarters.

Mandla is almost 60 miles, due south of Jabalpur, and served by first-class road and light railway. There is a fair weather motor road from Mandla to Khana in the centre of the valley.

Maps.—Splendid forest maps on the 4 inch to 1 mile scale made by the Forest Survey can be got from the Map Office, Dehra Dun. These show 25 feet contours, and, if desired, maps showing grass-lands, sal forest and mixed forests (Stock Maps) can be purchased.

Area.—From memory the area is about 40,000 acres, but for the purposes of a National Sanctuary some 30,000 additional and adjoining acres should be included. The Banjar Valley is merely a name given to a forest unit.

General Description.—Broadly speaking the area is a huge amphitheatre surrounded in a circular manner by a range of hills about 3,000 feet high. The bulk of the area is within these hills, but the forest extends down the outward slopes of the hills until the cultivated plains are reached. It is well watered throughout, but this of course could be improved, especially on the hill-tops.

The low-lying portions consist of grass maidans or open plains, young trees being cut back annually by frost. As soon as the contour above the frost level is reached pure Sal (*Shorea robusta*) forest is found. This, however, only extends a short way up the hillsides, where it gives place to the usual mixed forest of 200 or 300 species and bamboos. The rock and soil are metamorphic sand with occasional pockets of black cotton soil.

The Game.—In 1900 this tract contained as much game as any tract I ever saw in the best parts of Africa in 1908. I have seen 1,500 head consisting of 11 species in an evening's stroll. It is nothing like that now, but it is still probably true to say that it contains more numbers and more species than any other tract of its size in the whole of Asia.

Banjar Valley.

Game.—The following species are found in many numbers:

Bison	common	Nilgai	scattered
Swamp deer	common	Bear	common
Sambhar	common	Tiger	common
Chital	common	Leopard	common
Barking deer	common	Wild dog	common
Four-horned antelope	common	Hyaena	a few
		Jackal	common
Mouse deer	common (not often seen)	Fox	a few
		Porcupine	common
Black buck	two good herds	Pig	common

and a mass of small rodents and carnivora as well as Langur monkeys.

Chinkara are found on the outliers outside the reserve but rarely.

It will thus be seen that the tract contains all the game animals of the plains of India except chinkara, elephant, buffalo, lion. In 1900 elephants and buffaloes were regular rain visitors. The latter would probably return if given encouragement.

Legal Position.

This area is one of the oldest State reserves and belongs to Government. It contains valuable timber and is policed and administered by the Forest Department. Government would not care to give up working the valuable timber in the area, but this need not interfere with the Sanctuary.

It is essential that the area remain State Forest, otherwise the Forest Act would not apply. Also it is absolutely essential for our purposes that the Act should continue to apply. Some form of 'dedication' could no doubt adjust this as there is no incompatibility.

If the Act applies, as it must, and if the Forest Department continues to manage the Forest (timber), as it will, it is clear that our staff must be also the Forest Staff. Otherwise there will be two staffs in the same area, and one will be in opposition to the other. Moreover, the Forest Department has managed the game in India, against great difficulty, with signal success in most cases, and to deprive them of these functions would create resentment, especially, unless it could be shown to be reasonable and necessary.

Banjar Valley.

The shooting of game is strictly regulated, but a tremendous lot of poaching takes place. Part of it is always sanctuary, but these sanctuaries which are found in numbers in all districts are merely administrative shooting sanctuaries, resting blocks, pending opening to shooting again. They have nothing like the status of a National Sanctuary.

Some Suggestions.

The local Government might agree to the area being declared a National Sanctuary but would, I consider, be more inclined to give the proposal favourable consideration if it was initiated by Indian gentlemen. It might, therefore, be the best course to first obtain the support of the non-official members of the Legislative Council and it is believed that the conservation of Indian wild life for the benefit of the Indian People is a plea which no party can lightly thrust aside.

Conclusion.

I consider that action in India is urgently required, perhaps more so than in Africa. There are I know questions of detail which apply to particular areas and particular species which I have not touched upon but in the above I have attempted to tell you something about India as a whole, and in particular what definite action that might be taken in the Central Provinces.

No. 2. *THE BOMBAY PRESIDENCY.*

BY

G. MONTEATH, I.C.S.

It is five years since I left India, and a good many more since I was last in some of the Forest districts in which I have served. Those that I knew are all, with the exception of Thana, in the Central and Southern Divisions of the Presidency. Sind and Guzerat; Surat, the Panch Mahals, and the Dangs are 'terra incognita'. Anything I say therefore is subject to the qualification that my personal knowledge of conditions is limited to certain districts, and my experience hardly up to date.

In some Forest districts a heavy decrease in the numbers of certain species—those that afford, in addition to the sport of hunting them, desirable trophies—had taken place before the question of protection began to be considered seriously and rules were made under the Forest Act to impose some limit on killing. It must be admitted that up to that time—that is till after the beginning of this century—the main agent of destruction was the 'European' sportsman, to give him the title established by long usage in India. Neither the indigenous 'shikari' nor the wild dog—two kinds of 'poacher' frequently accused—can properly be blamed for it.

To take the villager first—his share of the damage done in the past in this part of India, where, as far as I have been able to find out, he has had no inducement of profit worth considering, is negligible, and his present activities hardly make enough impression by themselves to counterbalance the natural increase of the species he is generally concerned with. His usual method of hunting—a long and wearisome, and more often than not fruitless, watch by night, whether lawfully in his field or unlawfully and surreptitiously over water or a game-path in the adjoining forest—practically precludes such a result. He is little, if at all, more efficiently armed, and it is scarcely to be supposed that he is a better marksman or sees better at night, than his predecessors—most of whom, as Forsyth says, were bunglers at this kind of work. When a number of villagers combine, as they sometimes do—most often in my experience in the Kanara district—with nets or dogs or both, they may do a little better, but even these hunts are not on the whole, I think, much more productive of result than the solitary watch. The fact that they are illegal makes it necessary to keep them as dark as possible, and since they cannot be conducted without numbers and some noise, secrecy—unless there is connivance on the part of local subordinate officials—is not altogether easy. They do not therefore take place very often, and when they do the total result after a good deal of work, involving much careful preliminary investigation and placing of nets, hardly, according to my observation, warrants the conclusion that this kind of hunting causes any real decrease in the numbers of the species that is their main object—

in the Kanara district for our purposes cheetal, which seldom go far from the comparatively easily worked forests adjoining village sites. I say 'for our purposes' because I am dealing just now with forest species that are in need of protection. Pig of course are hunted too—pig and cheetal are the two kinds of forest dwellers that do most of the trespassing on cultivation that villagers complain about—but pig are prolific and in no need of protection—in Kanara perhaps rather the contrary. Cheetal also, if considerably less prolific, have still a natural rate of increase that would more than counterbalance the occasional killing of a few of them by villagers, as long as this was all they had to fear. Provided that due care and discrimination are exercised in the matter of gun licences for crop protection, there is not very much danger that the occasional unlawful use of a gun will do more harm than it has done in the past, and the evidence seems to show that this has been inconsiderable. In fact, if the grant of licences for smooth-bore guns—which are all that is needed for protection of crops, and all that villagers usually want (most often single-barelled ones and nearly always muzzle-loaders, for financial reasons)—is proportioned to the area of cultivation (and of course conditioned by the respectability of the individuals concerned), inhabitants of forest villages will do very well, other things being equal, if they hold their own against deer and pig. If sometimes for the sake of meat one or another of them sits up with his gun in a forest, or a number of the 'lads of the village' combine for a hunt with nets and spears (in this case usually their only armament, for guns are noisy and likely to be more dangerous to hunters than hunted) and they happen to be caught at it, I should be inclined to be lenient with them. After all it is arguable that the motive is as good a one as the desire for a trophy, which if the animal shot is a large one—say a bison—often involves, in Kanara at any rate, almost entire waste of the carcase.

Trade in hides and horns.

If there was money in it for the villagers, illicit hunting in Forest districts might be a more serious matter, but I never found much evidence of that kind of inducement. No doubt there has always been some illegal trade in 'Forest produce'—horns, hides, or meat for the purposes of this article—and no doubt it continues. Sambur leather I know is exported to England, but I do not think much, if any, of it comes from our part of India. I could never in fact discover that there was enough of this kind of trade in the districts I knew to matter very much—unlike some Provinces, to judge by what I have heard and read—or that most of what there was was done through the agency, or to the pecuniary advantage, of Forest villagers.

Protective Legislation.

However, such trade is admittedly illegal, and under modern conditions could increase very considerably in the absence of more effectual obstruction than seems to be possible at present, owing, I gather, to the interpretation so far allowed of the words 'Forest produce', which makes it incumbent on the prosecution to prove that any animal that is the subject of a case was actually killed in Government Forest. Certain animals are forest-dwellers whereever they may happen to be at the moment they are killed. It is not in this context the killing that is the offence, but commerce in certain kinds of 'Forest produce', an offence which by its nature is, in part at any rate, committed outside Forest limits. The contention that the particular animal in question was killed elsewhere than in Government Forest ought not in fact to be relevant. At least the burden of proving it should be on the defence (though I doubt whether that would get us much further). If an amendment of the definition is likely to be of use it would probably be easy to make it, but I think myself that what is wanted is legislation of a wider scope, to include animals that are normally found in non-forest country, for at the present time they are in a more parlous state than the others.

I said that up to date there was not much of this kind of trade in the Bombay Presidency, or rather that I had not seen much evidence of it up to the time when I left India. It has been a problem however in some other Provinces. I read for instance not long ago in the '*Field*' that in Assam similar difficulty of proving locality had been an obstacle in the way of effective protection of rhinoceros, for which there are sanctuaries. Under the conditions of today the question is quite likely to become a good deal more serious here than it is as yet, and steps ought to be taken in time—our present 'hunting and shooting' rules were made almost too late for some districts, and altogether too late to save certain species in them. It is not the local villager but a different kind of 'poacher' that we shall have to look out for, and it is I think about time to get ready for him. I will come back to him later.

Predatory Animals.

Before I go on I had better dispose as well as I can of the case against the wild dog, a very interesting creature with a bad name, for he shares in some degree with the inhabitants of villages in or adjacent to forest the odium of causing game to disappear faster than it can breed. There is a good deal of misapprehension about the actual amount of damage done by wild dogs, based partly on the impression they give of being much more numerous than they really are, and partly on the natural exasperation and prejudice caused by the fact that when the visit of a troop synchronises with that of a sportsman to a particular bit of jungle they undoubtedly often spoil the latter's chances, since the game is for the time being more or less disturbed, and the local tiger, finding his hunting interfered with, moves off. But a troop seldom remains in one place more than a few days. It makes its kill—with luck perhaps a second kill—and departs, and is seen again perhaps twenty miles away, creating the illusion that there are twice as many wild dogs in that area of forest as there really are. The game settles down again, the tiger returns, and the *status quo* is restored as soon as the dogs disappear, and it is a fact to be noticed that their most regular visits are to those places in which deer—their usual quarry—continue to be numerous.

Predatory wild animals do not, till man intervenes, increase out of proportion to their food-supply. Another thing to be borne in mind is the wild dog's method of hunting, which, like that of his co-accused the local villager, seems to me to settle the contention that he does enough damage to justify his proscription. The whole troop of dogs hunts one animal—most often a female or a young one—and sticks to the line (a pack of hounds might learn a lot from them) till that animal is run into, which may take half a day or longer. And a fair-sized troop hardly eats as much at a meal, so far as I have been able to observe, as one able-bodied tiger. I would do away with the price put on the wild dog's head—it is unnecessary for one thing, and for another I have never known it claimed. Instances could be given in support of what I have said, but this article is likely to be long enough without them.

I have argued this subject with Forest officers, some of whom were disinclined to agree, but it seemed to me that they had not thought much about it. I used myself to accept what was told me about the *'jugli kutta'* but long ago came to the conclusion that most of it was, to say the least, exaggerated. Certain Forest officers however of great experience did agree with the views I have just put forward—there is no harm in mentioning here that one of them is Mr. T. R. Bell, Late Chief Conservator of Forests, Bombay Presidency.

Local Conditions.

Some of the old books about 'Wild Sports' in India—classics of their kind—show how little the keen sportsman in the past, District officer, or soldier, or whatever his vocation might be, thought in the midst of comparative abundance about the future, and that the idea of protection of any kind—even of a close season other than what might be enforced by the season of the year—hardly occurred to him. Too often, as in Africa, he slew while he had the opportunity and spared not—(only in India we have not had the professional hunter). Even in Forsyth's time the result was beginning to be apparent, for 'now-a-days' he complains (writing of bison in Nimar as far as I remember—I am quoting from memory) 'a keen and active sportsman on a fortnight's leave would be lucky if he kept up his average for that period to one bison a day'. Fourteen in a fortnight—a poor bag! I do not know whether there are any bison left now in the Khandwa district—there are none in that part of Khandesh which adjoins it.

The aggregate of execution done in any area depended naturally on its accessibility from large cities, cantonments, or railway centres—in other words on the number of sportsmen that would visit it in a year. We have a good enough example in the Bombay

Presidency in a comparison of the state of things in North Kanara with that in Thana at the time when rules and a system of licensing were first put into force. In the latter district when I left it bison survived only in a small herd in one part of the forests, and today I am told are extinct: sambur were scarce: cheetal though pretty widely distributed were in small and scattered herds (and I need hardly say that their size generally indicates fairly well whether species that habitually go in herds are plentiful or not): the usually harmless bear, which, like bison, had been not uncommon twenty or thirty years previously, had disappeared altogether. Most parts of Thana, with its two main lines of railway and a sufficiency of tolerable roads, were easy enough of access in pre-motor days from Bombay, Poona, or one of the two or three hot-weather resorts on its borders, to make it worth while for any one with a taste for 'shikar' and only two or three days—say a week-end—to spare, to spend them on a shikar expedition in the Thana district. Kanara was a different proposition. Even after completion of the Southern Maratha Railway it took a good deal of time to get to Kanara for any one not resident in one of the adjoining districts, so that considerable preparation and 'bandobast' were necessary. Short expeditions repeated at more or less frequent intervals were consequently for most people out of the question. So when 'rules and regulations to govern hunting and shooting' were made there was still in Kanara plenty of game of all the species indigenous to it. It can hardly be argued that the local 'poacher' was so much less efficient in Kanara than in Thana as to account for the difference between the two districts, and the conclusion seems to be obvious.

Local Regulations: (1) *Southern Circle.*

The regulations in force in the Southern Forest Circle are in one main respect different from those governing the forest areas of the rest of the Presidency, in that the former include, and are in fact based on, the Central Provinces 'block' system. Mr. Bell and I drew them up in consultation, and they were sanctioned in the face of some opposition on the part of more than one Divisional Forest Officer, but I think Forest Officers in the Southern Circle would be sorry now to see the present system done away with and the old one reverted to. Elsewhere the views of those consulted prevailed, namely that the existing rules were good enough and the 'block' system was unnecessary and not easily workable in their circles.

That the present state of things in the Southern Circle forest areas is on the whole, as I think it is, satisfactory, is attributable mainly or very largely to the fact that the 'block' system and attendant rules were introduced in good time, that is before the general use of motor transport had begun to make many parts of North Kanara so much more accessible than they were in former days. The restrictions imposed by the old rules—consisting of little more than the necessity, for the purpose of shooting in Government forests, of buying a licence available for a year, and a limit of the number of head of certain species that might be shot by an individual licensee—would hardly have been enough by themselves to counteract the effect of a much greater annual influx of sportsmen, with the inveterate tendency of the majority to follow one another into well known and favoured localities. The system now in force seems to provide as adequately as any set of regulations can against overshooting of those parts of the Southern Circle forests to which it applies by means of a three-fold check. First the ordinary form of licence, that for a block, is valid for a certain period, during which the licensee has a virtual monopoly of that block. Secondly, there is the definite limit to the number of certain species that may be shot in a year by one licensee. The third and perhaps most important check is the limit to the number that may be shot in one block—it varies of course according to conditions, but when the number fixed for any block is reached in respect of a particular species no more of that species may be shot there for the rest of the year. These provisions seem sufficient to counteract over-shooting on licence. Obviously their effectiveness depends a good deal on co-operation on the part of sportsmen, for instance by reporting any cases noticed of unauthorised shooting or other breaches of the law and by furnishing correct returns of their own 'bag'. Such co-operation though occasionally an individual may be neglectful about his return, can for the most part be counted on.

All this has so far worked very successfully. The additional provision, by which certain blocks may be closed altogether to shooting for a series of years in a rotation which depends on the responsible Forest officer's observation of the stock of game completes the general measures for protection in the Southern Circle. In the result the position there seems, as I have said, to be on the whole satisfactory. Bison are apparently safe enough—they have nothing much to fear except rinderpest, and although at intervals they have suffered rather heavily from that, the intervals have been fairly long ones, and their numbers have been made up again, with the assistance of judicious closure, more rapidly than might have been expected. Sambur and cheetal are in little danger from the licensed sportsman, the indigenous shikari, or their natural four-footed enemies. I particularise these species because of forest species in the Bombay Presidency it seems to be they that chiefly require protection. Others are either not much sought after or are pretty well able to look after themselves, although I should like to put in a word for that interesting character the bear. I do not know that many bears are shot in the Southern Circle, perhaps not enough to warrant a limit being placed on the number assigned to a licence, but it is to be remembered that they were once fairly numerous in Thana and have disappeared from that district. They are nervous creatures and apt to be hasty in action if startled, but generally speaking do no harm. It is a suggestion which I put forward for what it may be worth. About elephants I do not feel myself qualified to make any suggestion at all. At present I believe there is *carte blanche* to shoot them, owing to their destructiveness to crops, a proposal to institute 'Kheddahs' or adopt some other means of capture having come to nothing. But it is likely that their case will sooner or later call for reconsideration. I do not believe that the total extent of their depredations is great, though of course that is no consolation to the individuals whose crops may happen to find favour with a herd.

It is unnecessary to go further into details in regard to the Southern Circle regulations, and in fact, though I helped to draw them up, my recollection of details is not very definite; but there is just one rule in which I should like to see an alteration made, namely that which lays down a fine for the killing by a licensee of a female of any of certain species. In practice, as far as I remember, the maximum fine was more often than not exacted in such cases. It is an irritating rule, and unnecessary in my opinion. Nobody shoots a female on purpose, and with species that ordinarily go about in herds marriageable females predominate so much over mature males that the occasional accidental killing of one of the former does no harm—it may indeed be beneficial, since the female killed in mistake for a male (it is most often a bison) is likely to be pretty well on in years. It seems unfair that an error of judgment that is practically innocuous and usually made known by the licensee's own report of it should involve a penalty—the maximum fine in many, if not most, cases—while the offence of unlicensed shooting goes so often unpunished because it cannot be brought home to the offender. It might very well be laid down that if a female of one of the 'scheduled' species is shot by a licensed sportsman and the fact duly reported, it should count as one of the number allowed by the licence. Such a provision would do no harm at all, and the sportsman would probably be more cautious in future about believing what his orderly or shikari told him.

(2) *Northern Circle.*

So much for the Southern Circle. The position, as was said above, is less satisfactory elsewhere. What it was like in Thana when I left that district—rather a long time ago—I have roughly indicated, and one can hardly suppose it has improved, regulations notwithstanding. Khandesh—or East Khandesh, the part I knew—was better off. The bison had gone, but there were plenty of sambur and, in practically the only locality in the district in which they are now found, there was a pretty good stock of cheetal. I believe at one time, not very long before I came to Khandesh, these had diminished considerably in numbers from over-shooting, but owing to measures taken by Mr. Simcox—a short open season, a limit of one head per licence, and the prohibition of any form of hunting other than stalking on foot, or, more accurately, 'still-hunting'—they recovered rapidly, and in a few years were again numerous. But I doubt whether measures that were ample for their purpose when horse-back, or that instrument of torture the Khandeshi 'chakra', was the sportsman's ordinary method of getting to his destination will be enough by themselves to prevent over-shooting in the future, now that it is easy to reach the chosen spot by motor car. It will probably be found necessary sooner or later here as in the Southern Circle to limit the total number of head that may be shot during the year, and the only way of enforcing such a limit seems to be the way in which it is done there. I have never been able to see any difficulty in using the same system that has proved its value in one part of the Presidency in any other district of it in which there is enough forest, and *ex hypothesi* enough forest fauna, to make rules of any kind for protection worth while at all. If the 'block' system can be worked in Khandwa it can equally well be worked in Khandesh, and unless it is introduced in Thana I doubt if effective protection is possible there. It may be admitted freely that the well-armed sportsman of today, 'European' or Indian, is usually, apart from legal restrictions, more moderate of his own accord than his predecessor, and that his presence is of definite assistance to the Forest officer in the latter's role of game-keeper. Nevertheless, whatever limits are laid down for the individual, their object is pretty certain to be defeated in the end by any considerable increase of the numbers that visit a given area, if there is no further check. It has proved to be the case elsewhere. If the Thana forests—to take that district alone—were divided up like those of Kanara it should be possible even now to increase the head of sambur and cheetal (bison I am afraid are past praying for) by systematic closure of a certain number of blocks in rotation, for as long in each case as the results observed from year to year showed to be necessary, the areas open to shooting having of course each its own annual limit as in the Southern Circle. An obvious advantage of the system over the old one is appreciable simplification for the already hard-worked Forest officials of the task of supervision.

With districts in the Northern Division other than Thana I have no acquaintance, but my impression is that they are not now-a-days much visited by non-resident sportsmen except for small game shooting. The existing rules may be enough in their case for the time being, but if at any future date the forest areas of these districts came more into favour with the seeker after larger game it would no doubt be well to make the changes just advocated for Thana and Khandesh.

Sanctuaries.

To sum up, the system of licensing that is in force in the Southern Circle having so far proved on the whole adequate there for its purpose, its extension to other parts of the Presidency where there are considerable tracts of forest in fairly regular request for shooting seems desirable. In fact I can see no other means at present available by which the gradual disappearance of the species most generally sought after may possibly be stayed, or the stock increased. Nor can I think of any further measures in supplement that would be feasible. The establishment, for instance, of sanctuaries on the lines of the African Game Reserves (but of necessity on a smaller scale), which I have seen advocated for some parts of India, and which may (though I doubt it) be a practical proposition for them, is manifestly out of the question for Bombay, and likely to be so for a long time to come. Expenditure on a special establishment to look after them could never be justified, and the burden of supervising much larger areas closed to shooting, which would consequently fall on the Forest staff, would be made no lighter for them—rather the contrary—by the absence as a matter of course of licensed sportsmen. Sanctuaries indeed other than those of manageable size provided under the rules by temporary closures of blocks, plus such natural ones as still exist in parts of different districts by reason of inaccessibility combined with climate, might very well in the end prove to be no sanctuaries at all.

Wild Animals in Non-Forest Areas.

If it may be granted that in some of the districts that have considerable areas of forest the state of the native fauna is not unsatisfactory, and in others of them is still capable of improvement, it is very different in the non-forest parts of the Presidency, that is of course in much the greater part of it. Antelope and gazelle (blackbuck and chinkara) when I left India had begun to disappear from many places where they used to be numerous, and doubtless the process continues. Here again local 'poachers' may be acquitted of blame, if one can call 'local' the peripatetic sort—Pardi, Haran-Shikari, or whatever his label. The ordinary villager seldom bothered his head about blackbuck, further than to scare them away from his crops. The others, from time immemorial, have wandered from one place to another—a gang of them does not want to camp long anywhere, and could not if it would, for they are 'criminal tribes' and the Police see to it that they move on. Their numbers are not large, and their painstaking method of snaring their quarry never produced results worth considering. They may do better with partridges and quail, or hares—I am inclined to think they do—but on the whole they can be counted out. Nor for that matter did the toll taken by the sportsman in the past affect perceptibly the stock of these species—blackbuck quickly learnt to adapt themselves to the range of improved weapons, and the chinkara is seldom an easy mark.

The extension of motor transport and the greatly increased number of licences for rifles are what has made the difference. The modern high-velocity magazine rifle of foreign make is cheap enough to be bought, even new, by many who could not have afforded the shorter-ranging express, and motor cars or cycles can go almost anywhere. Obviously any one who can own or part-own some kind of motor vehicle can also pay for a rifle—new or second-hand. He can often do so when he can only afford to travel by public conveyance.

Protection in Non-Forest Areas.

The difficulty of dealing with this comparatively recent departure is plain, and I must confess I can see no very efficacious way of doing it. Certain measures can of course, and should, be taken, but it is one thing to prescribe rules and penalties, and another to secure their operation, with no particular agency for the most part to rely on. Still, the knowledge that they exist might count for something.

So far little or nothing seems to have been done to limit killing of the species I am now considering. Yet they are clearly no less property of the State than the forest-dwelling species to protect which elaborate regulations are in force. The State is—in theory at least—the owner of all land in a rayatwari Province, with unimportant exceptions, and, as a corollary, of all game to be found on it. If indiscriminate slaughter of game animals elsewhere than in Government forests cannot be stopped altogether—and doubtless it cannot—yet it is time and more than time for some attempt to be made to delay its progress by rendering certain acts illegal.

A licence for the possession of a rifle can be granted for the purpose of self-protection, of crop-protection, or of sport, for all three purposes, or for any two of them. For self-protection a rifle is with rare exceptions unnecessary and unsuitable, and for crop-protection smooth-bore guns are the most that is needed. Remains sport. In the first place, then, when that is the ostensible object, the licence should prescribe certain definite restrictions on the species of game, and the number of each, allowed to the holder during the period for which it is available. The fee for it should be raised to an amount sufficient to emphasise its dual character—fire-arm and game licence: it should apply only to non-forest lands in the district for which it is issued, all fodder reserves or 'Kurans', whether in charge of Forest or of Revenue officials, being excluded: and the species allowed should be only those usually or frequently found outside the main forest tracts—in this Presidency blackbuck and chinkara, but not cheetal. Further, the licensee should be required, like the holder of a licence issued under the Forest Act, to furnish a return of what he has shot within the period of his licence. Such returns, on which very little reliance could be placed,—but they should be required all the same—could be rendered most conveniently perhaps to the Mamlatdars of the licensee's 'home' talukas.

So much for the licence to own a rifle (or gun) for sport, and the conditions to which it should be subject. The next thing to consider is the motor—privately owned, or public conveyance. It should be definitely forbidden, under pain of an adequate fine, to shoot from, or from the cover of, any kind of motor vehicle, and more especially to shoot by the aid of motor head-lights. I believe this prohibition already obtains in forest areas. The provision that no shooting at all should be allowed from or within a certain distance of a highway should be added in supplement, but it must be admitted that in any case, since cars can be—and are—taken over the roughest tracks across country, it would in practice be chiefly the users of public conveyances that these prohibitions would affect. Still, that would be something.

The last measure of those that I can think of is that to which I referred further back. The sale and purchase of meat or trophies of any kind of game animal, and not only such as can be brought within the definition of 'Forest produce', should be made illegal, and the penalty should be heavy enough to make both buyer and seller cautious. It goes without saying that the bribery of subordinate officials, by the present for instance of part of the meat of an animal shot, is 'illegal gratification', and it is equally clear that it is an offence nearly impossible to detect:—information offered by a jealous rival is about the only means by which it is ever brought to light.

The Motoring Poacher.

It was in this context that I mentioned that it was time to get ready for another kind of 'poacher'—one very different from and a good deal more efficient than the resident variety—and this brings me back to the forests, where he has already arrived, though he has not as yet perhaps done very much execution on the whole. The opening up by means of roads for the exploitation of timber of more and more of the high forest areas puts more and more places that were previously hardly accessible within reach of the man who can command the use of a motor car. So far not much advantage seems to have been taken by the unlicensed shikari of roads other than the main Public Works routes that run through forest land, and little damage has been done to species other than cheetal—the most 'get-at-able' for the motoring 'poacher'—but quite sufficient, I am told, to them in some places to give reason for anxiety. If he widens his sphere of operations by taking to Forest roads other species may suffer, but it should be easier to obstruct him here than on the public routes—he will be more noticeable and less mobile, and there is greater likelihood of his falling in with some of the Forest Staff. On the main roads I think the most that Forest officers can generally do is to keep these gentry moving, but the illegality of shooting without licence should be emphasised by adequate punishment of the offender when he does happen to be brought to book—including attachment of his gun or rifle, which may be unlicensed, or if licensed has probably been brought outside the district for which it is licensed. Ordinarily of course a licence to possess a rifle—or even gun—for sport should not be valid beyond the boundaries of the district in which it is sanctioned.

If distance and the offender's mobility combine to render the already hard-worked Forest official's task difficult in this respect by day, at night it will still more seldom be possible to catch the poacher in the act of poaching—he can get away too quickly. The most that can be done is to watch likely places for him at occasional and irregular intervals—a constant or regular patrol is out of the question—and trust that the knowledge that he may be looked out for, and if caught will be severely punished, will impair the accuracy of his aim. It must always be remembered that this sort of duty is not only arduous and discouraging in its results, but may at times be dangerous. It is a good deal to ask of a lonely Forest Guard that he should outbluff an armed and probably truculent man—perhaps two or three men—and he may well be excused if he sometimes looks the other way.

2

Agencies for the Protection of Wild Animals.

If things are thus difficult for the Forest staff in their domain it is clear that the Police—the only agency to all intents that we have in the very much larger non-forest areas—cannot be expected to do much in the way of enforcing the measures I have suggested. Inspection of fire-arms licences comes within the scope of their duties under the Arms Act, and that is almost all they can do. If a constable witnesses or is told of a breach of any of the rules—supposing that something like what I have indicated is done—he will, it may be hoped, report it, and the charge against the offender may be substantiated, but evasion is likely to be easy. The Police have too much to do otherwise for it to be possible to put any of them on special duty as gamekeepers. Local public opinion, what there is of it, will probably be on the side of the offender rather than of the law. If there were large zamindaris in this part of India the problem would be easier, for some measure of non-official assistance could then be looked for, and perhaps local associations formed, as I believe has been done elsewhere, but in a rayatwari Province very little of that sort of thing is possible. Neighbouring Rulers of States can no doubt be counted on to set an example, and jagirdars whose holdings are large enough to provide some measure of harbourage would in most cases be willing to co-operate to the best of their ability. For the rest, we shall probably have to wait till educated opinion—likely, one may hope, to be sympathetic but for the most part concentrated in the cities and towns—begins to influence the country-districts. By that time, it is to be feared, the herds of blackbuck and chinkara will have vanished from many places where they used to be a frequent and most pleasing sight.

However, the difficulty of enforcing measures is no argument against their being taken, if there is agreement about the object.

These species will not have been exterminated of course. Blackbuck when hard enough pressed take to the forests, and chinkara are always partly forest-dwellers, being found when undisturbed mostly on the border-line. In forest limits both can, like other species, find present sanctuary, and perhaps indulge the hope of returning some day to their old haunts. I said further back that the formation of larger sanctuaries than what the Forest Game laws afford, to be looked after by a special department, were out of the question in Bombay for financial reasons. I add here my definite opinion that for forest areas they are also unnecessary. The officers concerned have managed the laws for the protection of game in their own sphere of authority efficiently, and can be trusted to do so in the future, so long as their discretion is not unduly interfered with. The example of Africa, sometimes cited, is clearly no precedent for India—I need hardly set forth the reasons, for that would be to elucidate the obvious. The motor car is likely, it is true, to be an increasing embarrassment, but a special Game Department would be, as far as I can see, in no better case than the Forest staff for dealing with it. However, I am wandering into an academic discussion—a Game Department is anyhow not a practical proposition for Bombay.

If any rules and prohibitions on the lines of what I have suggested have been enacted already, or are in contemplation, I am sorry for my superfluousness, and can only plead that it is five years since I left India, and that I should have been glad if some one with up-to-date knowledge had been induced to write this article, instead of me. If not, I need only say that except on some such basis I can see no way of reducing even to a slight extent the super-abundance of fire-arm—and especially rifle—licences, or dealing with that infernal invention—how happy we were, game included, without it!—the motor car, and not even a distant hope of restoring to the country-side one of its most characteristic ornaments—blackbuck feeding confidently within view of the highway.

PRINTED AT THE DIOCESAN PRESS, MADRAS—1934. C9987

THE PRESERVATION OF WILD LIFE IN INDIA.

No. 3. *ASSAM.*

BY

A. J. W. MILROY.

(*Conservator of Forests, Assam*).

The question of affording adequate protection to game in Assam is a difficult one that we cannot expect will receive much local attention just now with so many important political changes staged for the immediate future, but in view of the imminence of these inevitable changes in administration it might be undesirable to postpone any longer the consideration of what system of preserving the fauna, whether the present one or something on different lines, will be most likely to survive the introduction of provincial autonomy.

Up to thirty years ago there were still very extensive unoccupied tracts in the Province, the first to disturb them being Gurkhali buffalo-keepers who began then to invade Assam with their herds, to be followed by ever-increasing hordes of immigrants, after the Brahmaputra Valley had become linked to Bengal by the railway.

Rules regarding close seasons had been framed at an early date for the Reserve Forests in conformity with practice in other parts of India, but game remained entirely unprotected in the waste lands known as Unclassed State Forests, until about 1910 when close seasons were introduced following a letter to *The Times* by Sir Harry Johnston on the indifference shown by Provincial Governments in India to the fate of their wild animals; but as no fees have ever been charged for shooting in the Unclassed Forests, there have been no funds for the maintenance of a special patrolling or protective staff, and the protection afforded by the rules alone has consequently been very meagre.

Types of Game Country.

Enormous areas of grass and reeds used to extend from the banks of the Brahmaputra towards the hills which enclose the valley on both sides, and it was here that most game used always to be found—rhinoceros, and swamp deer in the low-lying places, elephants, bison, and other deer nearer the hills—but these are precisely the very localities that attract the buffalo-herdsmen and the settlers, so that a great deal of this type of jungle has now disappeared for ever and it is only a matter of time before the most of the balance goes too. In these circumstances the policy adopted a few years ago of issuing gun-licences almost indiscriminately has only accelerated what was bound eventually to take place, and what has already occurred in all countries suffering from, or blessed (as the less far-sighted hold) with, an increasing human population.

Most of the former great shooting grounds are thus being occupied exclusively by Man and nothing can be done in them for wild animals. There remain for consideration the Reserve Forests, which have been taken up mostly for timber, but which include as Game Sanctuaries two important grassy areas.

Dense, evergreen forests contain comparatively little fodder suitable for game animals, which prefer the more open and the deciduous tree forests, but everywhere in Reserves reasonable game preservation should be looked for, seeing that the sale of shooting permits is a possible source of revenue, that rules exist for the benefit of the various species of animals, and that a Forest Staff is provided by Government to uphold these and other Forest Laws. It must be confessed, however, that in Assam just as in Burma, judging from some recent Annual Forest Administration Reports from that Province, game preservation is largely a matter of individual whim, and that encouraging results obtained by one Divisional Forest Officer are only too often dissipated during the regime of a successor, who is indifferent to this side of his multifarious duties.

The present Government cannot be accused of lack of keenness. Three years ago, a British Officer and a Company of Assam Rifles were detailed to spend six weeks touring a district where the inhabitants had got out of hand and were poaching in the Monas Game Sanctuary on a commercial scale, while at the present moment an energetic Assistant Conservator is on special duty at the head of an anti-poaching campaign that is doing some very good work indeed. The Assam Legislative Council have recently declared Rhinoceros horns to be forest produce wherever found, it has become much easier to deal into the trade in these, as horns are now liable to seizure unless their possession can be satisfactorily accounted for. No help from the centre, however, can make up for lack of interest on the part of the officers on the spot, though an enthusiastic Conservator can do much to overcome apathy, thanks to the tradition of loyalty in the Forest Service, but to be really effective he must possess both the time and the inclination to tour 'off the map' and away from the usual comfortable, stereotyped marching routes.

At the worst a certain amount of game of most sorts will linger on in the larger Reserves for some time yet, but not in the smaller ones which can be easily raided, and from which animals are always straying into settled lands bristling with guns: at the best, if the Forest Department does not depart from the policy of recent years as regards Forest Villages and as regards demanding the co-operation in these matters of its subordinates, quite a fair number (in some places sufficient to allow of restricted shikar) of the more interesting species will survive in suitable localities within the forest boundaries.

Increased pressure on the outside land being likely to lead to a demand for catastrophic disforestation of cultivable areas inside the Reserves, it would appear to be advisable to proceed cautiously, when and where needs be, with the formation of Forest Villages, especially of non-resident villages which luckily for wild animals are preferable from the utilitarian point of view, as they do not waste good forest land in hamlet sites and cattle-grazing grounds. Forest Officers in Assam will always be dependent on elephants for getting really inside their forests, and this again is lucky for the game, because it is essential permanently to set aside from settlement adequate and inviolable elephant grazing grounds while there is yet time; for want of which provident measure other Provinces have had to plant fodder at considerable expense for their Government elephants.

It would be illogical to allow villagers to grow crops in a forest and then to withhold from them the means of guarding the same, but the practice lately enforced of calling in guns for safe custody after the harvest is over is only logical and reasonable, and prevents the villagers from degenerating into professional poachers, as some of them have become in the past.

It had been intended, in order to obtain complete control, to acquire on behalf of Government all the guns owned by Forest Villagers for temporary issue at the right time, together with any others that might be necessary, but this measure has had to be postponed until funds become available again.

Game Sanctuaries.

The two Game Sanctuaries of which mention has been made are situated, the Monas towards the north-west on the Bhutan frontier and the Kazirunga in the centre of the valley on the south bank of the Brahmaputra. Both areas were originally selected for the Great One-horned Rhinoceros (*R. unicornis*) they contained, and a very fine stock of these animals was raised as the result of the protection afforded. Kazirunga, the more low-lying, is particularly suited for buffalo too, the Monas for bison along the Bhutan boundary.

The rhinoceros, our most important animal from the natural history point of view, is a difficult species to preserve even though its destruction is forbidden by law, because all parts of its body may be eaten even by Brahmins and because its horn is reputed throughout the East to possess aphrodisiac properties, while it lays itself open to easy slaughter by its habit of depositing dung on the same heap day after day. The demand for rhinoceros' horns has always been considerable in India, but of recent years China has also been in the market, consequent on the practical extermination of *R. sondaicus* in Lower Burma, Tenasserim, etc., with the result that a horn is now worth just about half its weight in gold. The prospect of a lucrative business led to an organization being formed for passing on rhinoceros' horns and elephant tusks to Calcutta, and the disturbed political conditions provided the virile Boro tribes (Meches and Kacharies) living near the Monas with the opportunity to take up poaching on a large scale.

The operations of the financiers in the background were checked for the time being; the advent of the Assam Rifles restored order;

additional game-watchers were engaged, and an Assistant Conservator was placed in charge of the Sanctuary to carry on the good work, but in view of what has happened in Burma, despite the best efforts of the authorities there, one cannot be confident that the fight we are putting up will not prove in the end to be a losing one if we merely continue on present lines.

A fundamental obstacle to success lies in the difficulty of identifying poachers unless these are actually caught in *flagrante delicto*, and this must always be a rare occurrence when members of a gang have only to separate and run a few yards into the high grass to evade capture.

Both Sanctuaries are at present inaccessible for want of roads and camping huts except to those who can travel light, such as poachers and game-watchers, and to those who can command the use of elephants, such as Forest Officers and a few planters. It was pointed out some years ago that this being so it would be quite possible, without the outside world being any the wiser at the time, for a dishonest subordinate in immediate charge of a Sanctuary to sell all the game while his Forest Officer, absorbed in other duties, was earning credit for the good work he might be doing elsewhere in the division. The loss would obviously be irreparable, and it was suggested that in these circumstances the western and eastern portions of the Monas Sanctuary, which with adjacent Reserves contains an effective area of about 150 sq. miles, should be opened to shooting under very strict supervision, the bag being limited (wounded to count as killed) and very high fees being charged, while the central part was preserved inviolate for the benefit of those interested in studying or photographing wild animals. The Sanctuary is only 10 miles north of the Amingaon branch of the Eastern Bengal Railway, and the interior could very cheaply be made accessible to lorries and cars running up from the station by constructing a few cold weather roads in flat country; the whole journey from Calcutta would take less than twenty-four hours of comfortable travel.

It was felt that in this way a healthy publicity would be ensured, because anyone coming up to shoot or to photograph would have plenty to say if game was found to be very scarce, also that the Sanctuary would be put on a paying basis, for whether the East actually is or is not less materialistic than the West, it is certain that no Province will be able to afford idealistic Finance Ministers, and finally it was felt that overstocking of the ground could in this way be guarded against.

It is permissible to believe that the Sanctuaries might have some chance of survival if they could be made more or less self-supporting, but precious little otherwise, and the question is one on which, we may feel sure, advice from the Society from the depths of its experience would not be resented. The Assam of the future may very well be proud to think it is taking its stand by the side of other civilized countries in saving its fauna from extinction, but it is going to be a poor Province, at any rate to start with, and if only some revenue could be expected from shooting permits and from the sale of captured specimens to Zoological Gardens, there would clearly be less initial hostility for the good cause to face.

Anything in the nature of a Public Park on the lines of the Kruger National Park would be out of the question unless it was under Imperial control because if the Assamese tax payer ever wants anything of this sort, he will certainly demand that all predatory and dangerous animals be removed before he disports himself in it.

Balipara Political Area.

Apart from the two Sanctuaries mentioned previously, the rhino have one remaining refuge, namely, the Balipara Political Area. Here some very valuable protection has been afforded to this animal in one area by a planter who is an enthusiastic game preserver. Efforts should be made now to enlist the sympathies of the authorities who will have to guard the welfare of frontier tracts for many years to come, and who will doubtless welcome more extended interest being taken in a matter that has now become of world-wide importance to naturalists.

The specially favourable factors in the case of the Balipara Political Area are:—

(1) It will permanently remain outside the influence of the new reforms.

(2) It consists very largely of Forest Reserves, which contain a number of rhino haunts, Gohpur, the Diputa, Gabharu, and Sonairupa rivers and, if buffalo-grazing was stopped, the Bor Dikrai.

(3) The tract is under a Political Officer who is provided with summary powers and the means of upholding them.

The possibilities here are obviously great, and the opportunity of achieving something permanent seems too good to be neglected.

Type of Game.

A few particulars regarding some of the species found in Assam are added by way of conclusion:—

Elephant (*E. maximus*). The country available for wild elephants has been much reduced as the result of land being taken up for settlement while the increasing unwillingness on the part of villagers to tolerate damage to crops will prevent any slowing down of catching operations, but elephants will continue to be numerous in several districts for a long time yet. Over 400 were caught three seasons ago by the Forest Department in one area alone, but this was probably the last big Kheddah that the Province will ever see. Casualties used to be heavy during training, but Government took the matter up and has demonstrated that these are unnecessary and that much higher profits follow the adoption of more humane methods. The rumour that a dumpy breed of wild elephant lived on the central ridge of the Garo Hills has been found to be false as regards the existence of herds composed of such animals, but the inquiry showed that exceptionally short-legged specimens are to be met with; it is a matter that some local officer might find interesting to pursue further.

One result of the decrease in the number of wild elephants is the inconvenience experienced in getting about Reserves where elephants have become scarce, as their paths are no longer kept open by the passage of herds. The Province of Bihar has always been the best customer for elephants but as it will be out of this market for many years to come, it is not improbable that elephant control measures will have to be undertaken as in Burma.

The Great One-horned Rhinoceros (*R. unicornis*) has been dealt with already at sufficient length.

The Smaller One-horned Rhinoceros (*R. sondaicus*).—It is on record that Messrs. Rowland Ward identified the head and shield from a rhino shot by a Forest Officer in the Bengal Dooars as belonging to this species, and it would be strange if it did not also occur in the contiguous Goalpara Reserves and Monas Sanctuary. Pairs of smaller, less truculent, and definitely less armoured rhino can be put up in the Sanctuary and these, if not cases of *R. unicornis* pairing while still far from mature, must be specimens of *R. sondaicus*.

Investigation into this is most desirable, and perhaps the Society could arrange for it being carried out in the course of time. The Kacharies recognize three varieties of rhino, and though their classification is not made on scientific lines, it does not follow therefrom that it is all moonshine.

The Sumatran Two-horned Rhinoceros (*R. sumatrensis*).—Formerly common in the Luhsai and Manipur Hills and occasionally found in North Cachar, but by now almost hunted to the vanishing point by Lushais and Kukis. The opening up by forest villagers of several big patches of marshy land in the Forest Reserves of South Cachar seriously reduced the number of suitable haunts available for this species. Most of the remaining patches, however, will have to be kept closed to cultivation in order to preserve feeding-grounds for the timber-dragging elephants, and some special steps have already been taken to try and look after the few rhino still left alive in this difficult country where little control can be exercised over shikaries. The record flood of July, 1929, drove the rhino up into the hills and very few have been allowed by the Lushais to return.

The Indian Buffalo (*Bubalus bubalis*).—The great-horned variety, *macroceros*, formerly existed on the Monas, but had been practically shot out before the formation of the Sanctuary. The writer was fortunate enough to meet the last survivor, a well-known cow, at least a hand higher than the ordinary sized bull with which she was consorting. The Vernay-Fanthorpe Expedition searched for this cow unsuccessfully, and she was never seen afterwards. The best heads come from Central Assam, so there should be some very fine specimens in the adjacent Kazirunga Sanctuary.

The Assamese utilize the services of solitary wild bulls for their domestic cow-buffaloes, a magnificent breed which is bound to deteriorate now that wild bulls are getting scarce, and in the absence of anyone interested in scientific breeding. Buffaloes with wild blood in them live longer and are finer draught animals than those of inferior strains, and the cows give more milk. Their disadvantages are sensitiveness to sun and bad tempers.

The wild and tame buffalo of the marshes live largely on the wild rice-plant and are accustomed to warm wallows, but the wild buffalo of the upper reaches of the Monas feed on highland grasses and bathe daily in the cold river water which would be fatal to the marsh-dwellers. These upland buffalo are possibly a little higher on the leg.

The wild buffalo in the Diyung Valley of the North Cachar Hills are very distinctive with short legs, great barrels, and straight horns without the backward sweep before coming forward again to form the tips. Many Mikir Buffaloes ran wild about 1897, when their owners had died from Kala-azar, but probably the whole stock had tame ancestors as they closely resemble the so-called 'Manipuri Buffalo' which is brought through Manipur from Burma for sale in the Surma Valley.

The Gaur (*Bibos gaurus*).—Just as the buffalo is having a bad time from everyone wanting to grow rice where it wants to live, so the gaur, though safe from the Hindu and living in hills in which shifting cultivation alone is practised, is suffering from the hillmen, who sit up at night over saltlicks and plug everything that comes along; consequently it is already only a tradition in many hills where formerly numerous, solitary bison bulls breed with the tame gayals or Mithun (*Bibos frontalis*) in the neighbourhood of the Kutcha Naga villages in North Cachar and consequently the tame animals there are coloured the same as the wild ones, but wherever there has not been any infiltration of wild blood for a long time, as in the Abor Hills and parts of Manipur, albinism in varying degree is common, many Mithun being pied like Friesian cattle.

A Kachari gamekeeper, a bold man not given to romancing but also not infallible, declares that he has encountered and is scared of a larger, redder, fiercer Mithun to be found at a few places on the Bhutan border, and the same story is told by the Mikirs in the hills on the Kamrup-Nowgong border away on the south bank. This may have something to do with the alleged large 'Moh-mithun' and smaller 'Goru-mithun' of the Assamese Plains. The writer before he had heard about the supposed red variety was once eating his breakfast at dawn on a cliff while camp was being struck, while two bull Mithun were mooning about in the rocky riverbed below. One, as ascertained by glasses, was young but was as big as the old black fellow; the young one was very markedly red even to the naked eye at a range of 500 or 600 yds., and was either a freak in colour or else belonged to a separate variety, associating perhaps with one of the black kind after having been driven out from its own herd. Circumstances always arose to prevent the fruition of the expeditions planned to investigate the matter but as there is some possibility, if not probability, about the story being true, it is to be hoped that somebody will one day be able to find time to go and camp in those parts and inquire.

4

Swamp Deer, Barasingha (*Rucervus duvaucelii*).—This beautiful deer will soon only be found within protected areas. as it is so easily shot by poachers using elephants in their business. The horns in Assam are poor.

Sambar, Hog Deer, and Barking Deer (*Rusa unicolor, Hyelaphus porcinus, Muntiacus muntjak*) are all common in Assam. The sambar is the big-bodied, solitary Malayan type with small antlers; both sexes display that extraordinary raw patch on the lower side of the neck, for which no reasonable explanation has been suggested. Specimens reared in captivity do not develop it.

The Indian Wild Boar (*Sus cristatus*) is abundant and still interbreeds with village pigs. These without occasional crossing with the wild stock often develop white patches, like the tame Mithun, either in the form of blazes or white socks.

Pigmy Hog (*Porcula salvania*).—Not uncommon in places but seldom seems to be shot.

Wild Dog (*Cuon rutilans*?).—All villagers and many Europeans in Assam assert that there are two kinds of wild dog, a larger species hunting in packs. The writer had only come across the latter once and so long ago that he was beginning to think he must have been mistaken until an opportunity occurred a couple of years ago on the Barak in Manipur to observe this small variety at close range. A sambar hind was standing in the water staring into a little hidden bay and occasionally stamping her foot. While the boat was paddled quietly up the pool a wild dog appeared on the bank, apparently to act as sentry, and not noticing the boat at once it proceeded to perch itself on a rock. It was not only considerably smaller and more foxy looking about the ears and muzzle than the familiar wild dog, but in place of the rather short thick tail it had a regular brush, which it curled gracefully forward just as a fox would do when sitting down. There were about a dozen of these dogs round the corner worrying the skin of a sambar fawn, which had been devoured before the very eyes of the mother standing less than 30 ft. away. This was being discussed one day at a station on the hill-section of the Assam-Bengal Railway called Harangajao when a Gurkhali herdsman chipped in to say that both varieties of wild dog killed cattle of his during the Rains: he distinguished them as Hindu and Mussulman dogs. A good reward was promised if he would bring in skins and skulls of both kinds, but without any result.

The most interesting bird that Assam can boast of is the Pink-headed Duck (*Rhodonessa caryophyllacea* Latham), which is possibly extinct elsewhere. There were a good few at one time in some lagoons known to the writer and a few friends, but their number was unfortunately thinned out by a baboo doctor posted in the locality in connection with Kala-azar duty, who was the possessor of a gun and, if he liked eating these duck, of a most indiscriminating palate. The jungle which protects the lagoons is gradually being cleared away and with it the last of the duck is likely to disappear.

No. 4. *THE UNITED PROVINCES.*

BY

F. W. CHAMPION, I.F.S.

(*Deputy Conservator of Forests, United Provinces*).

One among the numerous striking results of the Great War has been an awakening all over the world to the fact that wild animals are tending to become less and less in numbers in many countries, and often species that were common a few decades ago are being, or actually have been, entirely exterminated. Most of us who went through the War saw far too much of killing ever to want to see any more, and the natural reaction has been that a new spirit of sympathy with wild creatures has become firmly established in many countries. Wild life protection societies are springing up here and there, particularly in America and England, and the Society for the Protection of the Fauna of the Empire is doing great work in trying to preserve the wonderful fauna of the British Empire from further wanton destruction. An enthusiastic branch of this Society has been started in India and a very good work is being done, but unfortunately it is not receiving so much support from Indians as could be desired. Indians, many of whom are prohibited by their religion from taking life, should be the very first to support such a Society and a number are already whole-heartedly doing so, but real mass support has yet to be received. This I believe to be very largely due to lack of knowledge of the aims and objects of such a society, and insufficient propaganda, and I am confident that much greater support will be received in future as a result of the great efforts now being made by the Bombay Natural History Society and the various local branches of the Society for the Preservation of the Fauna of the Empire, which all who have the slightest interest in wild animals should join without a day's further delay. After all, once a species of wild animal has been exterminated, no money, no Society, no human agency can bring that species back to the world, and delay in helping those who are doing their best to save species already threatened with extermination may mean that help, tardily given, is given too late.

Position of Wild life.

The present position in the United Provinces is, perhaps, not quite so bad as in some other parts of India, owing to the presence of a very sympathetic government, an influential Forest Department, and great land-holders, all of whom have always remembered that, within limits, wild creatures have just as much right to exist as the human race. The position inside reserved forests and in certain large estates, which is fairly satisfactory, will be discussed later in this article, but first the present state of affairs in the ordinary districts will be considered. It is the conditions in these ordinary districts, composing 80 per cent or more of the whole Province, which are causing so much worry to those who are interested in wild life. Frankly the position is appalling. The vast increase in gun-licenses which has taken place within recent years, combined with the greatly improved means of transport, has caused a drain on the wild life of the districts such as can end only in the almost complete destruction of any kind of wild creature considered to be worth powder and shot. Laws do exist imposing close seasons, but these laws often are not, and cannot be, observed in present-day conditions. Deputy Commissioners and Superintendents of Police in some cases do their utmost, but they are so over-worked nowadays with political and economical troubles that, however keen they may be, they literally have neither the time nor the energy to try to enforce unpopular laws, which, by comparison with present-day troubles, possibly do not seem very important. Further the responsible officers in a district are very few in number and it is quite impossible for them to stop bribery among their often low-paid subordinates. A rupee or two or a piece of meat is quite sufficient temptation to an underpaid *chowkidar* not to report an offence under a Wild Animals' Protection Act, particularly as it is often extremely difficult to prove such an offence, and, even if proved, a subordinate magistrate will generally let off the offender with a purely nominal fine. It therefore seems that, in the present state of the country, any Act enforcing close seasons outside Reserved Forests, however well it may be conceived, is worth little more than the paper on which it is written. In actual fact special efforts are now being made in Hamirpur and Meerut districts to protect *sambar* and *chital*, but it is not known to the writer how far such efforts are proving successful. Animals like black-buck and *chital* and game-birds, both in the plains and particularly the hills, are literally being wiped out at an increasingly rapid rate and one wonders if there will be anything left except monkeys and jackals after another two or three decades. There is one bright spot, however, and that is that non-game birds at least are not harried to the same extent as in England because the egg-collector is scarce, and the average Indian boy, unlike his English confrere, does not amuse himself by collecting vast numbers of birds' eggs, only to throw them away in most cases as soon as the boy begins to grow up. Taken as a whole there is no doubt whatever but that the position in these plains districts of the United Provinces is just about as bad as it could be, but one must always remember that these areas are very densely populated and that really there is not very much room for any considerable numbers of the larger game animals, which must tend to interfere with the cultivator and his crops. In any case leopards are found in many places, since they are prolific breeders and very difficult to keep in check, and, even if more adequate protection were given to the game animals in cultivated districts, it is probable that their numbers would still be kept down by a corresponding increase in the numbers of leopards.

Sufficient has now been written to show that the position in the cultivated districts is very unsatisfactory, but that increasing population in already heavily populated areas, combined with the present political and economic distress, makes it very difficult to make practical suggestions for improving matters. What can be done is for large land-holders in sparsely populated districts to preserve restricted areas really efficiently and noble examples of what a great help to the wild life of a country such measures can prove to be is to be found in the great swamp-deer preserves of Oudh, notably those of the Mahrani Saheba of Singahi and of Captain Lionel Hearsey. The former of these has been under careful protection for many years and an area of perhaps 20 square miles now contains several thousand head of these magnificent deer. A few are shot annually, but the number destroyed is almost certainly less than the natural increase, and these public-spirited benefactors can justifiably feel that, so long as they maintain their present standard of efficient preservation, there is no fear of the swamp-deer following the already long list of fine animals which have been exterminated from the United Provinces.

Reserved Forests.

Now the position of wild animals in the Reserved Forests, of which the writer, being a Forest Officer, has perhaps a specialised knowledge, will be considered. Firstly the writer would state most emphatically that United Provinces forest officers as a class are, and always have been, extremely sympathetic towards wild animals. Few are really heavy killers and quite a number do not shoot animals at all, beyond their requirements for food for themselves or their camp followers. An odd individual here and there, both in the present day and in the past, has possibly let his sporting instincts drive him into becoming a really heavy killer, but the amount of slaughter done by the average forest officer in these Provinces is conspicuously small. It sometimes happens that disgruntled sportsmen state that Forest Officers are selfish or destroy more animals than all other classes put together; but these statements are most emphatically untrue and generally have an inner history, which reveals the accuser as having some personal grudge against an individual Forest Officer, which leads him to make general insinuations which are totally unfounded. None could be keener on the preservation of wild life than the present writer, and, if he thought that his brother officers were indifferent to the preservation of wild animals, he would not hesitate to say so. The writer believes that it would be a great mistake to remove the wild animals inside Reserved Forests from the protection of the Forest Department and place them in charge of a separate Game Department. The present system is working very well and such action would be regarded as a slur on Forest Officers and would alienate the all-important sympathy of the powerful Forest Department.

The United Provinces reserved forests are not very extensive and they are all under the personal supervision of divisional forest officers. Poaching does occur to a limited extent, particularly during the monsoon when the forests have to be deserted owing to their unhealthiness, and from motor cars, but such poaching is not very extensive and every effort is made to keep it in check. Elaborate rules, which are constantly being amended, do exist for the issue for shooting licenses, for the enforcement of close seasons, and for helping any species which is tending to become scarce. These rules may not be perfect—no rules ever are—but at least their object is to provide shooting for all who apply in the right way, and at the same time to preserve the wild animals in perpetuity without letting them increase to such an extent as to become a nuisance to forest management or to surrounding villagers. Species that, for any particular reason, need help are entirely protected, examples being wild elephants for many years and Sambar in Lansdowne division since an attack of rinderpest in 1927; and senior forest officers are always ready to listen sympathetically to applications for protecting particular animals in particular tracts. Even tigers now have a close season and are not allowed to be shot by artificial light. Some may argue that it is a wrong policy to protect tigers, but at least such protection shows that forest officers consider that even tigers have the right to live in their own jungles.

On the other hand some wild animals, such as deer, do seriously interfere with the management and revenue of valuable forests, and the forest officer cannot allow deer to increase to an excessive extent. In some cases, particularly where the balance of nature has been upset by the excessive destruction of carnivora, deer have become a positive pest, and it has proved necessary to reduce their numbers. Or again, the proportion of hinds may have become excessive, with consequent deterioration in the size of the stags, so that some of the hinds have had to be shot off; but such destruction is stopped as soon as the position becomes normal once again. It is true that individual forest officers, keen silviculturists who have found all their efforts at improving the forests ruined, have occasionally advocated the total destruction of deer; but it is not the general opinion that such drastic measures are required and interesting experiments are now in progress by which considerable areas, in which plantations or efforts at obtaining natural regeneration of valuable trees are in progress, are entirely closed with game-proof fencing, which keeps out the deer. Such fences are somewhat expensive in initial cost, but they can be moved from place to place as required and are probably the best solution for managing forests both in the interest of the forester and also of the indigenous wild life.

It is sometimes stated that, even in the reserved forests, wild animals are much scarcer than they used to be. The writer cannot speak for 30 or 40 years ago since the old records are not clear and he was not in India at that time; but, even if the head of game had diminished, it is possible that the numbers were excessive in the past or that the memories of those who claim that animals are disappearing are a little at fault. After all, most of us tend to think of the 'good old times', although it is possible that those times were not quite so good as they now appear in perspective. An effort has been made to collect figures of animals shot in the past with those shot nowadays for comparison, but records of 30 or 40 years ago do not give the information required. The following are the conclusions that the writer draws from the figures that are available:—

(a) Taken as a whole the head of game shot recently has generally not shown any marked decrease, except in the mountain reserved forests, where control is not so easy.

(b) Tigers appear to have increased and marked decreases seem to have taken place in the numbers of *nilgai*, *kakar*, wild-dog and black-buck. The decreases are partly due to serious floods and rinderpest epidemics, and are probably natural fluctuations which will right themselves in time. Wild-dogs have decreased owing to the large reward paid for their destruction.

(c) The decreases in the number of some animals shot recently are due to the removal of rewards as a measure of economy.

(d) It must always be remembered, however, that the number of animals inside Reserved Forests is probably being artificially swelled by the influx of refugees from the appalling conditions at present prevailing outside. This influx will decrease as animals outside become exterminated. Also modern rifles are so good and shooting with the help of a motor-car is so easy, that probably a greater proportion of the existing animal population is shot annually nowadays than was the case in the past.

(e) The Forest Department watches these lists carefully and takes action whenever such action appears to be required.

(f) The general impression of senior forest-officers is that, although there have been considerable fluctuations in particular areas, the game in the United Provinces Reserved Forests as a whole has not markedly decreased during the last 25 years, except in the high hill forests.

To summarise, the present position of wild animals inside the Reserved Forests of the plains and foot-hills of the United Provinces does not give cause for serious anxiety, except for the ever-increasing use of that arch enemy of the wild animal—the motor car. The numbers of wild animals in the mountain reserved forests appear definitely to be decreasing. The position in some zemindari estates is good and in others poorer; and the position in the ordinary districts is almost hopeless.

Some Suggestions.

The writer would make the following suggestions to help the present state of affairs:—

(a) *Public opinion.*—This is by far the most important of all methods of wild life conservation, and, without it, all efforts to preserve wild creatures will prove abortive. Good work is already being done by propaganda and by lectures, but much more remains to be done. Good illustrated books help greatly and the formation of sanctuaries and national parks, where the general public can see wild animals in their natural state, would all help. Major Corbett as local Secretary of the United Provinces branch of the Preservation of the Fauna of the Empire Society is doing a lot to assist in this work.

(b) *Laws.*—It is much easier in the present state of India to pass a law than to see it enforced, but the writer would greatly like to see laws passed on the following points:—

(1) *Sale of shikar meat, trophies, etc.*—It is of vital importance that a law be passed at an early date totally forbidding the sale of any portion of a wild animal, with certain definite exceptions. Such exceptions would be the dropped horns of deer, and the hides of deer where numbers have to be reduced. Special licences should be issued in such cases and such licences, liable to cancellation at any moment, should be under the personal control of the Divisional Forest Officers, where reserved forests are anywhere near, or under Deputy Commissioners where there are no forest officers. The sale of any *shikar* trophy should be entirely and absolutely prohibited. Such a law, properly enforced, would finish the professional poacher, and would end the nefarious dealings of certain taxidermists who sell *shikar* trophies to those 'sportsmen' who are incapable of bagging anything themselves.

(2) *Limitation of gun licences.*—This is very difficult in the present political state of the country, but at least greater efforts could be made to differentiate between game licences and licences for the protection of the crops, person, property or display. Gun licences for the protection of crops should insist that barrels should be sawn-off short, as such licences are very largely applied for when the real object is poaching.

(3) *Motor cars (and also carts and tongas).*—The shooting of any wild animal from, or within, say, 400 yards of a motor-car, cart or tonga, either by day or by night, should be made an offence liable to prosecution. The writer personally would like to stop motor cars altogether from entering Reserved Forests, or, where this cannot be done, he would like to place check-chowkies at the entrances and exits of such roads, the cost to be covered by a small wheel-tax. Fire-arms would either have to be deposited at such *chowkies* or would be sealed, so that they could not be used while inside the forests. The excuse of requiring fire-arms for protection en route should not be accepted, as passengers in motor-cars very rarely need protection from wild animals, except possibly from occasional rogue elephants or man-eaters. Luckily recent economies have resulted in the abandoning of some of the motor-roads in the Reserved Forests of the United Provinces. The writer would like to see them all abandoned! The old time *shikari* or Forest Officer managed perfectly well without them, and they tend only too often to make his modern successor slap-dash and lazy.

(4) *Protection of rare stragglers.*—It occasionally happens that a rare animal, such as a rhinoceros, strays into Reserved Forests from Nepal or elsewhere. Such animals should be rigidly protected with a fine of, say, Rs. 2,000, or imprisonment, for their destruction. The excuse that 'If I don't shoot it, someone else will' should never be accepted in such cases. The recent law passed in Bengal for the protection of the rhinoceros, should be extended to the whole of India.

(5) *Rewards.*—The writer considers that Government rewards

for destroying wild animals should be given far more sparingly than in the past. Luckily, recent economies have resulted in a great reduction in the rewards offered, and it is sincerely to be hoped that such reduction will be permanent. Rewards in the past have encouraged poachers and have sometimes caused an upset in the balance of nature where they were misapplied. They are really quite unnecessary except for man-eaters and notoriously destructive creatures such as porcupines.

It has been suggested that details of breeding-seasons of various animals should be appended to this article. Inside Reserved Forests every effort is made to protect wild creatures during their breeding seasons and nothing more can be done. Outside Reserved Forests, as already explained in this article, the position is such that protection can very doubtfully be enforced. Hence such an addition to an article which is already too long seems unnecessary, but the writer can supply a list of breeding seasons, so far as they are known, to anyone who is specially interested in the matter.

Since writing the above I have been reconsidering this question and have read up a certain amount of literature on the subject. On the whole I have little to add to what I wrote before except that I am not so certain as I was that the head of game inside the United Provinces' reserved forests is not decreasing. I was posted to N. Kheri Division in 1921 and I returned there again in 1931. Although still a good place for animals in 1931, I would estimate that there had been at least a 25 per cent decrease in nearly all species during that decade. The reasons for this reduction I would put down to (*a*) Motor-cars making shooting far easier than it used to be, (*b*) the destruction of game in the adjoining areas outside the forests resulting in a smaller influx and greater damage to animals straying outside.

I am now in Bahraich division in Oudh, which has a reputation of being a good game division. I have now been here for 5 months and, so far, I have found game of all kinds to be rather scarce, although I hear that more animals come in from Nepal in the hot weather. The reasons for this apparent decrease are the same as in Kheri, i.e., motor-cars and destruction of animals outside the forests, combined with increased poaching along and near the Nepal border.

I have recently heard from Col. A. E. Wood, I.M.S.—a keen supporter of the Darjeeling Natural History Society—that in his earlier days Lachiwala in Dehra Dun division used to be a 'veritable paradise' for wild animals. I am well acquainted with Lachiwala and I can only say that it is very far from being an animal paradise nowadays. It is more a 'paradise' for motor-picnicers from Dehra Dun City and Cantonment!

On the whole I am afraid that there is a distinct doubt that the game inside the reserved forests—particularly in Oudh, where motors now penetrate to every corner—is so plentiful as it was, although the present position does not give rise to the same anxiety as is the case with other areas not under the control of the Forest Department.

PRINTED AT THE DIOCESAN PRESS, MADRAS—1934. C885.

THE PRESERVATION OF WILD LIFE IN INDIA.

No. 5. THE INDIAN LION.

BY

SIR PATRICK CADELL, KT., C.S.I., C.I.E.

I have been asked by the Honorary Secretary of the Bombay Natural History Society to write a note upon the Indian Lion, and the measures needed for his preservation. I gladly do so because I believe that there is no other wild animal in India which could so easily become totally extinct. It is now preserved solely by the efforts of one State. Should that State for any reason become weary of well doing, the lion would disappear from India in two or three years.

It is not necessary to write at length upon the history of the Indian lion. Two excellent articles on the Kathiawar Lion, written by Lieut.-Colonel Fenton, will be found in the Society's *Journal* of April 1909 and January 1911, and a chapter on the Indian Lion, which summarises most of the available knowledge, may be read in Brigadier General R. G. Burton's *Book of the Tiger.* It is sufficient to say that the lion was once widely distributed over India. Less than one hundred years ago it was common round about Delhi, and it was not very uncommon in Central India and Guzerat not more than seventy years ago. At about the same period it was to be found in the Barda Hills of Jamnagar and Porbandar, while it remained in the Girnar Range near Junagadh City till 1879. Now, however, the lion is entirely confined to the Gir Forest of the Junagadh State. That forest does not extend to 1,500 square miles, as Colonel Fenton says, but to 494 square miles only. The former figure once correctly represented its dimensions, and the late Maharaja Jam Saheb Ranjitsinhji, who spent a good deal of his boyhood within the limits of Junagadh, told me that he had then heard of lions in areas now distant from the forest. The spread of cultivation has very seriously encroached upon the forest and if this encroachment has now been stopped, it has largely been for the sake of the lions. Every one will agree that five hundred square miles is not a great area for the preservation of a species, and, alas, it has not proved to be large enough to prevent the animals straying into other jurisdictions where they have been of late years somewhat ruthlessly shot down.

It should be noted that it has long been recognised that the lion would disappear without preservation, and that it was believed that even with such preservation its extinction could only be postponed. Colonel J. W. Watson, an excellent observer and shikari, when writing the statistical account of Junagadh for the Bombay District Gazetteer about 1880, stated that 'there are probably not more than ten or a dozen lions and lionesses left in the whole Gir Forest', and this in spite of the statement that these are strictly preserved'. When Lord Curzon proposed to visit the Gir to shoot a lion, a well known Bombay citizen, who happened to be visiting Junagadh, wrote to a Bombay paper pointing out that there were supposed to be less than a dozen animals surviving. Immediately Lord Curzon was informed of this, he cancelled his shoot, and advised the Junagadh Darbar to preserve the animals strictly. Colonel Fenton writing in November 1908 states that the preservation was not very strict and that the animal was 'slowly but surely approaching extinction' and again that it was 'fast disappearing'.

It was, I believe, entirely owing to the fact that there was a British Administration in the State from 1911 to 1920 with a much stricter preservation of the lion and a considerable amount of co-operation for the time being from neighbouring jurisdictions that the lion has survived, and to some extent increased in numbers.

One of the dangers of the extinction of the lion lies in the comparative ease with which it is shot, and its lack of cunning and finesse as compared with the tiger or the panther. Before I explain the circumstances which make it easy to shoot, I should perhaps state my own qualifications for offering an opinion. I have never drawn a bead upon a lion, but I have been present when some have been shot by State guests. I have also seen lionesses come to tie-ups when a lion was sought by such guests, and have had several tie-ups and beats purely for purposes of observation, and not for shooting. I have of course discussed the matter with local shikaris and others who have seen many lions killed.

The reasons why the lion is a much easier animal to bring to bag than the tiger or the panther are as follows: In the first place, the lion is, as Colonel Fenton points out, a much noisier animal. He will constantly give away his presence by roaring, which a tiger or a panther does not do except for special reasons. Secondly he is in much more open country, especially in the hot weather. The reader of Colonel Fenton's articles will notice that in several cases he was able to stalk lions under trees, and to fire at them when they were resting or lying down. Such a process would be practically impossible with the tiger or panther. Thirdly the lion is much more sociable, and moves about in troops, often comprising three generations. This may not make it easier to shoot a particular animal, but it does make it far easier for the sportsman who is not very particular, to get something, even if it is only a lioness or a half-grown cub. Fourthly the lion, or at least the lioness, if one or more is accompanying the lion, comes out far more readily to a tie-up. In the case of a very good lion, shot two years ago by a visitor from England, the lion came out almost immediately in broad daylight to a goat tied in the open when there had been no previous kill. It is true that, when there are lionesses, the lion, or the principal lion, seems to prefer to send them out first, either to spy out the ground, or to do the work of killing, or perhaps from the more gentlemanly motive of giving the lady the first morsel. In at least three cases, I have known the lioness to come out and do the killing, while the lion has kept in the background throughout. In another case the lioness did a long stalk towards the tie-up, a young buffalo, through a cotton field, and finally lay down within a few yards of it, without attacking it, presumably waiting for the assistance of the lion. She was, however, more patient than we were, and we had to frighten her away when we got down. In a recent case, the lion did come first, and made no attempts to kill, and the lioness came out afterwards and did the killing: but she was a young animal, and the lion seemed to watch her performance with benevolent interest. It is usual to tie-up for lions in the day-time both a goat and young buffalo. The goat is invariably taken first because, as the shikaris say, the lions want to tackle the more serious problem of the buffalo in quiet. Panthers do, of course, occasionally come to tie-ups with extraordinary boldness, but they do not often come, unless they have already killed at the place, with such openness and in such broad daylight as the lions do.

My experience of drives for lions is small, but I should say that, while the lion comes rather faster than the tiger generally does, he gives more notice of his approach, and avoids the open spaces less than a tiger would do. He consequently gives an easier shot.

An obvious cause of their undoing is the confidence of the lions. When they know that they are not often interfered with, they naturally appear more boldly in the open. A good instance of this occurred at our Christmas Camp last year. A lady and a man were riding with an orderly in the afternoon. The lady, riding ahead, came sharply round a corner on a forest road on to a lioness rolling in the dust of the road. The lioness got up, went to the side of the road, and stood there while the riders went past. The remarkable thing was that while the lady's horse started slightly, the other two did not seem to see or mind the lioness. The animal was almost certainly one that we saw in a beat two days later, a very fine lioness of a much more golden colour than is usual with the Kathiawar animal. In another case, a family of lions allowed the inmates of a car to get out and take some cinema photographs of them without any uneasiness.

It is obvious that an animal so easily brought to hand could only be kept extant by strict preservation. This was applied, so far as the Junagadh State is concerned, during the period of Administration, and has since been maintained by His Highness the Nawab of Junagadh. During the Administration, not even a Governor of Bombay, for whom the shooting of a Kathiawar lion had become almost a hereditary 'hukk', was invited to shoot in the Forest. Unfortunately, though the true Gir Forest lies almost wholly within Junagadh limits, the borders of it extend into at least five jurisdictions. At first, with the cordial help of the Agent to the Governor in Kathiawar, the other jurisdictions readily assisted in the work of preservation. The Darbar of one large State agreed originally to drive back into Junagadh limits any lions that strayed across. This abnegation proved too trying for a British Officer who shot several of such animals: but even then it was agreed that only male lions that were actually doing damage should be shot. Now, however, any such restriction seems to have gone by the board.

Lions require a particular environment as a breeding haunt and it is believed that there are no suitable areas outside Junagadh territory. But the animals are easily enticed across the boundary by a succession of tie-ups. It is not only the rulers or officials of these jurisdictions that shoot the animals, but the practice has now begun in one jurisdiction at least of inviting guests from long distances to shoot the lions. One of these guests assured me that he only enjoyed watching the animals. This may have been his only enjoyment, but I was afterwards told that he had shot a young lion and two lionesses. To our certain knowledge, because the news of the slaying of an animal rapidly spreads, twenty-two animals have been so slain within the three seasons ending in 1934. There may have been more but there certainly have not been less. Now it must be agreed that the lions do stray voluntarily, apart from enticement. This occurs particularly during the rains, when insects are bad in the Gir. At that time, however, there is little shooting. Doubtless, however, the lions do damage occasionally: but they would easily be frightened away, if the full-grown males were shot, and no great damage would be done to the stock of lions thereby. No such restriction is observed in practice. Perhaps because, as I have noted above, lionesses and half-grown cubs come most readily to the tie-ups, nearly all of the twenty-two animals I have referred to have belonged to these categories. In one case five animals, none so far as I could ascertain of full size, were shot by the young members of one family. In another, four animals, a young lion, two lionesses and a cub were practically ringed in, and were slain, all the four being claimed as falling to the rifle of one young sportsman.

I believe that it is sometimes suggested that the Junagadh State is selfish in trying to restrict, and, as it is alleged, reserve for itself the shooting of lions. If this is so, the selfishness is not personal. His Highness the Nawab, though a keen rifle shot, has shot only one lion during the fourteen years that have passed since he assumed the Government of the State. There is not an official in the State who has fired at a lion. If every year the State has the very real honour and pleasure of entertaining distinguished guests for a lion shoot, it is a distinction which costs a good many thousands of rupees. There is also the steady annual cost of the sums paid in compensation to villagers and herdsmen whose cattle have been killed by lions. When the State hears of people being invited from afar to shoot the lions bred in its limits it cannot be a matter of surprise if the game sometimes seems hardly worth the candle.

I am often asked how many lions still remain in the Gir. As I have said above, there were supposed to be less than a dozen in 1880, and about the same at the beginning of the century when Lord Curzon's visit was cancelled. As a result of the strict preservation during the Administration the number was believed to have increased to fifty, though even in those days poaching was not unknown. It has since been stated in the London *Times*, and the statement is quoted in General Burton's book, that there are now two hundred lions. I believe this number to be greatly exaggerated. The fact that lions move in troops, and that they cover long distances leads to over estimation. If a man sees a troop of six or seven animals, and hears of a similar number some miles away within a few days, he naturally fixes too high a number for the whole forest. My own opinion though it is only a guess is that there are not much more than 75 to 80. It is obvious that this number cannot stand a drain of ten or twelve being shot yearly, especially if the animals so killed outside Junagadh limits are all of young breeding stock.

It may be observed that there is no real excuse for shooting a lioness in mistake for a lion. Even if the shooting of female tigers and panthers were regarded as being unsportsmanlike and reprehensible, the sportsman might well plead that he had not sufficient time, or sufficient knowledge, to distinguish. But he could not truthfully say so in the case of the lioness. A lion which is not easily distinguishable as being such, must be very young and worthless as a trophy to the self-respecting sportsman.

What then is the remedy to be adopted against unfair or unwise shooting? It has been recently proposed in a high official quarter that all the jurisdictions concerned, that is all those which possess or border upon any portion of the Gir Forest, should agree to refrain from shooting within a mile from the boundary of another jurisdiction, and from shooting any but full-grown males. This would lead to some improvement though in two recent cases the condition that the animal shot should be a full-grown male has been, I am informed, somewhat liberally interpreted. But it may be doubted whether this is enough, and I venture to think that it would be better to come to an agreement that the total number of lions to be shot in one year should not exceed some such figure as five or six.

The pressure on Junagadh of suggestions for invitations to shoot lions is, it may be observed, increasing year by year, and the Junagadh Darbar would gladly welcome some such limitation. Unless an agreement is reached, and is faithfully observed, the danger of the disappearance of the lion from the fauna of India, and consequently from its last home in Asia, is obvious.

No. 6. WILD LIFE PROTECTION IN BURMA.

BY

H. C. Smith,

Deputy Conservator of Forests, Honorary Game Warden.

I. The Need for Protection.

General.

Most civilised Western nations have now realised what Burma has yet to learn, namely, that the perpetuation of an indigenous fauna is essential for a country's welfare.

The perpetuation of wild life is impossible under modern conditions without the enforcement of protective legislation. Burma unfortunately has as yet failed to realise the necessity for such protection and unless she takes immediate and vigorous steps to cast off the apathy which up till now has characterised the attitude of her general public towards all matters pertaining to the perpetuation of wild life she will most certainly be too late as irreparable damage will have been done.

Endowed by nature with a wild fauna which in variety, beauty and interest compares most favourably with that of any country in the world it is the bounden duty of the present generation to hand it down to posterity in as complete a form as possible.

In the early stages of the Province's development wild animals and birds of all kinds were plentiful, guns were few and consequently there was little need for elaborate protective legislation or at any rate for its rigid enforcement.

Recent years, however, have seen a marked change in conditions generally, communications have been improved; more country has been opened up; cultivation has been extended, curtailing the area available for occupation by wild life; and an enormous increase in the number of firearms throughout the province has resulted in the indiscriminate slaughter of numerous kinds of animals and birds, especially in the more accessible districts.

Development must, of course, continue and wild life must, just as inevitably, recede before it, but, in a country like Burma, there is no reason why the indigenous animals should not be perpetuated for all time in certain areas without their presence in any way impeding future national progress. Such animals as tigers, elephants and *thamin* are entirely out of place, and their presence cannot be tolerated in the immediate vicinity of human dwellings or intensive cultivation, but in most of the reserved forests of the country their existence is not only welcome but must be considered an important national asset. Wild animals may be destructive to crops but they are generally harmless to man unless man attacks them first and wounds them. Even a tiger except in the rare cases in which he has turned man-eater goes out of his way to avoid man, and people with a true knowledge of the jungle pay very little attention to his presence unless he starts raiding their cattle.

The main reason why so little interest has up till now been taken in the protection of Burma's fauna is undoubtedly that most people are extremely ignorant on the subject. They do not realise that the possession of a number of wild animals and birds is a very valuable asset to the province nor do they realise that the stock cannot last for ever unless certain restrictions are imposed on its destruction.

To the jungle Burman all ideas of protection are not unnaturally entirely foreign and he instinctively looks for guidance in such matters to the educated classes. If, therefore, the latter fail to set the correct example he can scarcely be blamed for his irregularities.

The average villager has always been accustomed to obtain plenty of everything with very little trouble and is quite oblivious of the fact that supplies must soon come to an end unless their use is systematically controlled.

Bamboos, houseposts, thatching, firewood and water he has always been able to get with ease close to his village. Paddy he has been able to grow with the minimum amount of exertion and wild animals and birds he has regarded as things to be killed whenever possible either to provide meat or else because they damage his crops.

It is extraordinarily difficult to make the villager realise that if he goes on wastefully cutting timber and fuel according to no plan there will soon come a time when the supply will run out and either he or his descendants will suffer in consequence.

One of the main duties of educated Burmans should therefore be to help villagers to realise that with the spread of development and increase in population the time has come when the unrestricted exploitation of all kinds of forest produce cannot be tolerated.

Wild animals and birds are a very valuable form of forest produce and need to be conserved every bit as much as bamboos, timber and fuel.

If only people from Burma could see for themselves the conditions existing in parts of India and other countries where development has already advanced much further than it has at present in Burma and note the distress which has been caused by the wholesale destruction of forests and all that they contain, they would most certainly wake up and take steps now lest the countryside of Burma should share a similar fate.

While it should be a comparatively simple matter to make the villager understand the necessity for the maintenance of a continuous supply of timber, fuel and bamboos, it may not be quite so easy to persuade him that the preservation of a stock of wild beasts is equally advantageous.

Certain wild animals have from time immemorial damaged his crops, killed his cattle and at times also endangered his life and he has therefore, grown up to regard them as his natural enemies to be killed whenever and however possible. Other wild creatures, though quite harmless, he has regarded as meat, of which he has always tried to obtain as much as possible in the easiest way.

Reasons why Wild Life should be protected.

In any country the perpetuation of an indigenous fauna is necessary for commercial, agricultural, scientific, aesthetic and sporting reasons. In Burma the precepts of the Buddhist religion must surely provide an additional cause for protection.

A large portion of Burma's wealth is derived from timber which cannot be economically extracted without elephants. These animals cannot live for ever and a supply of wild elephants must always be maintained from which the domestic herds can be replenished and increased as trade expands.

A considerable amount of revenue is realised annually on account of license fees and royalty paid on the collection of various parts and products of wild animals. There is no reason why this revenue should not be greatly increased with careful management without the fauna being in any way adversely affected.

An immense amount of good is done by many kinds of birds by destroying insects and other pests which would otherwise prey upon crops, domestic animals or human beings. Woodpeckers, owls, nightjars, egrets, drongos, rollers and mynas, are particularly useful in this respect.

A vast amount of information of use to science has been acquired in the past from the study of wild animals and a great deal more awaits discovery. The stocks of specimens in museums throughout the world will not last indefinitely and must therefore be periodically replenished.

Most wild animals and birds add very considerably to the beauty and interest of a countryside by their presence A country devoid of all wild life, is unnatural, and under such conditions the national character must be adversely affected.

The study of the habits and ways of wild creatures provides one of the healthiest and most beneficial forms of amusement for the people and needs all possible encouragement. Townspeople have few opportunities to study wild animals in their native haunts and have therefore to be content to do so in Zoological Gardens and National Parks. These institutions are increasing in popularity all over the world and their stocks of wild animals and birds will require periodical replenishment.

The pursuit of certain wild creatures *in strict accordance with the dictates of sport* provides one of the finest forms of training for the country's youth and of recreation for its manhood. Individual skill and physical prowess are involved in the location and coming to close quarters with most kinds of wild animals. Perseverance, patience, ability to overcome hardship and difficulty, power of endurance and mental and physical fitness are all virtues which are cultivated and fostered by the pursuit of wild beasts and since these are the qualities which go to make the ideal citizen or soldier every effort should be made to induce the youth of the country to acquire them.

It is the overtaking and the outwitting of an animal which provide the training and the recreation and it matters little whether observation, photography or killing is the ultimate object. To Buddhists whose religion forbids them to take life the first two objects will naturally appeal whilst others will probably wish to kill to obtain a trophy.

II. Legislation.

Existing Legislation.

The legislation at present in force for the protection of the fauna of Burma consists of the following:—

(i) The Burma Game Rules, 1927, together with certain notifications and special orders issued under them. These are all issued under the authority of the Burma Forest Act, 1902.

(ii) The Wild Birds and Animals Protection Act, 1912, which applies to the whole of British India.

(iii) The Indian Arms Act which provides for the control of guns and cartridges used against wild animals and which is also an all-India Act.

These laws together with certain other matters of interest to sportsmen are contained in a *Burma Game Manual* which is on sale to the general public at a price of twelve annas.

Also, since the regulations have necessarily been written in much detail and in legal phraseology which may not be readily understandable to some, an abstract containing their salient points but having no legal significance has been compiled. This abstract which is in the form of a pamphlet entitled *Game Law in Burma* has been prepared in both English and Burmese for general circulation *gratis* in the Districts.

The existing laws whilst making adequate provision for the destruction of wild animals which are a menace to human life and property, for the obtaining of scientific specimens and for the killing of game for sport should, if only they are enforced, afford reasonable protection to the fauna of the Province.

In *bona fide* defence of life or property any person may kill a wild animal in any way he pleases.

The killing of game for the purpose of sport is controlled by the issue of game licenses, particulars of which can be obtained from any Divisional Forest Officer.

It is illegal to hunt any kind of wild animal or bird inside a reserve forest or game sanctuary without a game license.

All wild animals and birds except the following, namely rhinoceros, tapir, buffalo, *mythun*, elephant, bison, *saing*, serow, goral, Argus pheasant, bittern, crane, drongo, egret, heron, hornbill, kingfisher, nightjar, oriole, owl, roller, stork, tern and woodpecker may be hunted anywhere outside reserved forests and game sanctuaries without a license but subject to the conditions of the schedule of close seasons which is reproduced in full below:—

THE SCHEDULE OF CLOSE SEASONS.

No one may hunt any animal or bird mentioned in column 1 of this Schedule during the period mentioned as its close season in column 2 whether inside or outside a reserved forest with or without a license.

1.	2.
Males and Females of:— Rhinoceros, Tapir, Buffalo, *Mythun* Females of:— Elephant, Bison, *Saing*, *Thamin*, Hog Deer, Sambhur Males of:— All species of deer, if hornless or with horns in velvet.	... The whole year.
Males and Females of:— Serow, Goral, *Gyi*	... 1st July to 31st October.

Species	Close season
The Argus pheasant and all species of:— Bittern, Crane, Drongo, Egret, Heron, Hornbill, Kingfisher, Nightjar, Oriole, Owl, Roller, Stork, Tern, Woodpecker	... The whole year.
All species of:— Peafowl, Pheasant (other than Argus pheasant), Partridge, Painted Snipe, Plover, Quail	... 1st March to 31st August.
All species of:— Jungle Fowl	... 1st April to 30th September.
The Masked Finfoot and all species of:— Duck, Teal, Moorhen, Jacana, Watercock, Grebe	... 1st May to 31st August.

Note—(i) Special licenses are issued for kheddah operations.

(ii) Immature males of elephant, bison and *saing* may not be hunted at any time.

Mature males are defined as follows:—

Elephant.—Either tusk measured along the outer curve must project at least thirty inches from the gum or must exceed fourteen inches in girth.

Bison.—The horn must measure at least twenty-two inches along the outer curve or must show clearly defined transverse corrugations extending for at least four inches from the base.

Saing.—The horn must measure at least twenty inches along the outer curve or must show clearly defined transverse corrugations extending for at least four inches from the base.

Under Rule 4 of the Burma Game Rules certain methods of hunting are prohibited and except when animals are actually menacing human life or property no one may—

(*a*) shoot any animal with poisoned arrows;
(*b*) lay down poison for any animal;
(*c*) net wild water birds;
(*d*) hunt any animal by means of pitfalls;
(*e*) hunt within one hundred yards of the compound of a Buddhist monastery;
(*f*) hunt any animal during the period shown to be a close time for that animal;
(*g*) shoot any animal other than carnivora from any platform or machan;
(*h*) use artificial light for the purpose of hunting any animals other than carnivora;
(*i*) shoot animals other than carnivora from the back of an elephant or from any kind of vehicle;
(*j*) sell or buy, or offer to sell or buy or possess or destroy the eggs of any of the birds mentioned in the schedule at any time of the year; and
(*k*) hunt any animal named in the schedule for purposes of trade except elephants which are hunted in accordance with a special license.

Under Section 3 (b) of the Wild Birds and Animals Protection Act, it is unlawful in respect of any wild bird or animal for which a close season has been declared in the schedule of close seasons, to sell or buy or offer to sell or buy or to possess any such bird or animal which has not been captured or killed before the commencement of such close time, or the flesh or any other part thereof.

Under the Indian Arms Act it is illegal for anyone to lend a gun or rifle or supply cartridges to any person unauthorised to possess them.

Revision.

In 1925 in view of the increasing number of firearms and the development of the country, the Game Rules then in force were found to be inadequate to safeguard the fauna against serious depletion. A thorough revision of the Game Rules was considered necessary and the appointment of a Game Warden was found to be essential for the proper protection of the wild fauna. The Game Rules and the special orders and circulars under these rules were accordingly revised; the capture and control of wild elephants were systematized and a Game Warden was appointed.

The Burma Game Rules, 1927, came into force on the 1st November of that year and it was laid down that they should be revised after five years. They are now due for revision and since there are many points requiring consideration the matter should receive attention as soon as possible. At the same time, all existing legislation for the protection of the fauna should be thoroughly scrutinized by a body of men representative of commerce, agriculture, forestry, science, sport, religion and aesthetics.

A revision of the Game Rules will entail, amongst other things re-editing the *Burma Game Manual*, the Game Law pamphlets and the various Game licence forms, all of which work should be undertaken by a whole-time Game Warden who at present does not exist.

In 1931 as a measure of retrenchment the post of Game Warden was suspended. Financial stringency cannot justify such a retrograde step in regard to a post on which the total annual expenditure was approximately £1,000 irrespective of compensating revenue.

The rehabilitation of the post of Game Warden is essential if the progress made with wild life protection during the past five years is to be maintained.

A Wild Life Protection Act for Burma.

The Burma Forest Act of 1902, under the authority of which the Burma Game Rules, 1927, are issued only applies to reserved forests and public forest land. It is not applicable to private land.

The Wild Birds and Animals Protection Act, 1912, an all-India Act, applies to private land but no particular class of officer is responsible for its enforcement.

These two disadvantages were fully realised in 1926 when a new draft Act for Burma incorporating the pertinent portions of both the above Acts was drawn up, but never pressed for in the then newly constituted Legislative Council. The need for such an act has not lessened during the past five years and the Burma Game Rules and Wild Birds and Animals Protection Act should now be replaced by a special Wild Life Protection Act for Burma.

Necessary Amendments.

During the past five years a number of weak points in the existing rules have been shown up and certain amendments deserving consideration have been proposed. At the time of revision all criticism whether it be of a constructive or destructive nature should be carefully considered by a representative body.

The most urgent requirement at the moment is legislation to control the exposure for sale or barter of all wild animals or birds or parts thereof at all times and in all places. Until such legislation is introduced and enforced it will be practically impossible to prevent the netting and snaring of wild fowl for trade purposes which is carried on extensively to the accompaniment of great cruelty.

The schedule of close seasons requires careful scrutiny mainly with a view to removing petty inconveniences to sportsmen and making things still simpler for the uneducated.

Close times have been fixed so as to coincide as far as possible with the breeding seasons of the scheduled animals and birds using a minimum number of dates to avoid unnecessary complication and with due consideration for the requirements of sportsmen. In Burma, where certain animals breed the whole year round and birds of one kind or another lay their eggs in every month of the year, the compilation of an effective schedule on these lines is not easy.

The young of Barking Deer (*gyi*) may be born in any month and so these animals were given an arbitrary close season from the 1st of July to the 31st of October, this being the period during which it was thought that fewest sportsmen would be in the jungle. It now appears that many people like to spend their October holidays shooting and are inconvenienced, probably unnecessarily, by October being a closed month for *gyi*. If the existing close season for the males and females of serow, goral and *gyi* were altered to the 15th June to 30th September, many sportsmen would be satisfied whilst the animals in question would be none the worse off.

In 1926 the list of birds included in the schedule underwent close scrutiny and was considerably simplified, nevertheless, further modification is now necessary. The list, which as it now stands, includes approximately 260 species and sub-species, should again be carefully scrutinised by a representative body. An authoritative list of the Burmese names of all scheduled birds should be compiled.

In addition to the above proposals a number of minor amendments have been suggested many of which deal with technical points in connection with the administration of the rules. All these should receive due consideration as soon as a Game Warden and a representative body competent to deal with the situation can be appointed.

The Enforcement of the Laws.

In the past, the non-enforcement of certain protective measures was, to a certain extent, justified by conditions prevailing at the time, but now it is necessary to emphasize the fact that nothing short of a very strict observance of all such legislation in future can save the fauna from serious depletion and the province from a lasting reproach in consequence.

It is, of course, unreasonable to suppose that laws which have hitherto not been strictly enforced can all at once be enforced or that the apathy which has uptill now characterised the attitude of the general public towards Wild Life Protection can, at a moment's notice, be converted into an enthusiasm for the furtherance of such a cause. Nevertheless, it is hoped that when the change in conditions is realised the whole community will take up wholeheartedly the question of the protection of its wild fauna.

In Burma the executive department so far as the protection of the fauna is concerned is the Forest Department and Forest Officers supervise the regulations for the protection of Wild Life in their jurisdictions to the extent to which they take an interest in the matter and have the time to do so. This position may be unsatisfactory but, under existing conditions, it is possibly the best that can be attained.

A Forest Officer's duties give him exceptional opportunities for observing the conditions relating to wild life and for developing a sympathetic interest in the preservation of the wild fauna. It might be supposed, therefore, that the Forest Department would contain a large proportion of field naturalists and lovers of nature yet the hard fact is that only a small percentage of Forest Officers have anything but a superficial knowledge of the fauna in their forests or evince any real enthusiasm for affording it adequate protection. Naturalistic ability and interest in the wild fauna are not part of the compulsory equipment of Forest Officers and a progressive policy in respect of Wild Life Protection involves additional work which is neglected by a larger proportion of the Forest Establishment than might be expected.

In the majority of cases the local heads of Forest Circles and Divisions in common with many senior officials of other Government Departments, are men from overseas whose interest in handing down to posterity an undepleted fauna can in no way approach the viewpoint of the average colonial. This migrant official personnel to whom is entrusted the control of all matters affecting the fauna, however conscientious it may be in regard to the work for which it has been trained, cannot as a whole, raise sufficient enthusiasm over an optional interest in a country in which it has no intention to settle permanently.

Modern conditions of service have aggravated the situation and there is a growing tendency amongst officials to dissociate themselves from any but those matters which are part and parcel of their contracts and agreements. Increased office work often makes it impossible for district officials to spend sufficient time on tour and Forest Officers, with many special duties to perform in connection with their appointments, cannot usually devote sufficient time to the supervision of regulations for the protection of wild life which is frequently in parts of the country where forestry operations are practically non-existent. Leisurely touring in remote areas, which is so essential for effective Wild Life Protection and also incidentally, for the proper administration of a district, is no longer encouraged.

Within the last three years the situation has been further aggravated by the rebellion in Lower Burma and the economic crisis which has affected the whole Province. During the rebellion general lawlessness prevailed throughout several districts and in some forests it has only recently been possible to resume normal touring. The financial crisis led to a substantial reduction in the Forest Establishment and to an amalgamation of certain Forest Circles and Divisions. During this retrenchment Wild Life Protection received little consideration with the result that certain Divisional Forest Officers now find that it is quite impossible to enforce protective legislation throughout the vast areas under their charge.

The officers of the Forest Department are most directly concerned with the enforcement of the Game Laws but it is obvious that no matter how enthusiastic they may be, their efforts must be largely nullified unless they receive strong support from members of other departments and the general public as well.

Isolated individual efforts can achieve little in a case like this; what is required is a concerted effort on the part of every one for the attainment of the common end.

At present an active form of public opinion in favour of Wild Life Protection which plays such an important part in the enforcement of the laws in Western countries, is almost entirely lacking in Burma, and until it is created it is unlikely that a great deal of progress will be made. Its creation, however, should not prove a difficult matter if every sportsman in the country would make up his mind once and for all to adhere rigidly to the letter of the Law himself and make a determined effort to see that his subordinates and followers do the same. If all such men would learn to regard the non-observance of the Game Laws as unsporting and those who infringe them as persons not playing the game the desired form of public opinion would soon be created.

Ignorance of the necessity for protective legislation and even of its existence has undoubtedly often been the cause of numerous infringements in the past, but in these days there can be little excuse for a serious breach of the law at any rate on the part of an educated person.

Under existing conditions the killing of wild animals and birds for food alone cannot be justified, for when due allowance is made for the numbers which must be killed annually in defence of life and property, properly regulated shooting for sport is all that can be tolerated. These facts have been given due weight in the compilation of the existing laws, and if only these are strictly observed there need be little fear of any species ever being irreparably reduced in numbers.

Breaches of the Laws.

The practices of lending out guns and disregarding the close seasons, above all others are responsible for most harm to the fauna.

Many persons possess guns which they have little desire or ability to use themselves but they are nevertheless very fond of meat. They, therefore, lend their weapons to others to procure meat for them. The persons thus employed usually have little regard for the age or sex of their victims and pay little heed to the game laws or the dictates of sport.

The lending of a gun or rifle or giving of cartridges to persons unauthorised to possess them are practices which, besides being illegal, dangerous and unsportsmanlike, are, more than any others hostile to the cause of Wild Life Protection

In respect of the disregard for the close seasons the plea is frequently brought forward that men who are compelled to spend most of their time in the jungle should be allowed a certain amount of licence regarding the observance of the Game Laws. This is all very well, but in Burma no kind of Game exists in such numbers that its destruction purely for food purposes in contravention of the game laws can be justified,

If every one who earned his living in the jungle was allowed to obtain as much meat as he liked in any way he liked, then the wild fauna would very soon be exterminated.

In addition to lending out guns and non-observance of the close seasons there are other factors the effects of which, though not so far reaching, nevertheless form a considerable menace to the wild life of the country.

Recent years have seen a very large increase in the numbers of domestic cattle owned mainly by Indians. The herds in places have assumed large proportions, and containing as they do numerous weak and sickly animals they foster the spread of cattle disease besides consuming well nigh the entire food supply which belongs legitimately to the draught cattle of the local villages and the indigenous fauna. Every hot weather large numbers of *saing* and other wild animals succumb to disease which apparently originates with domestic cattle, and unless steps are taken to restrict the numbers and wanderings of the prolific herds, many of which appear to serve no useful purpose, considerable harm is likely to result.

Among a certain class of *shikari* the shooting of deer, pig and even *saing* and bison by lying in wait for them in *machans* or in 'hides' built near salt-licks, waterholes, wallows and game tracks is most popular. By this method at certain seasons of the year great destruction can be done, and if the method were to be consistently employed on a large scale game could be practically wiped out of most areas without much difficulty. In a country like Burma which carries such a very small head of game per square mile and in which for several months of the year animals are compelled through scarcity of water and fodder to concentrate round certain definite spots, such a method can never be permitted without the fauna suffering irreparable loss in consequence. Determined efforts are therefore needed to put a stop to these practices and to strengthen public opinion against them.

The shooting of *thamin* from carts and of other animals from the back of an elephant are practices which cannot be permitted. *Thamin*, in certain areas, can be approached comparatively easily in a cart, and most animals will allow an elephant with a man on its back to get to within shooting range before making off, with the result that by the adoption of such methods they can be easily killed.

A modern invention which is instrumental in the destruction of large numbers of hog-deer and to a lesser extent of other animals throughout the province is the electric torch. Its comparatively small cost and the ease with which it can be obtained has placed this article within the reach of all who can handle a gun and the damage which is now being done with it is very considerable. A deer when feeding out in the open at night can be located at a long distance with the aid of a powerful torch and the animal being apparently stupefied will allow the 'sportsman' to walk to within easy gun-shot range of it before making off. The result of this is that fields and open spaces are patrolled at night by men armed with torches and guns, and as many as half a dozen deer are often accounted for by one gun, in a single night. Needless to say, the shooter does not trouble himself about the sex or age of his victims. Many kinds of animals are killed with the aid of torches, but hog-deer probably suffer most.

In certain districts the low-lying areas along the banks of the big rivers become flooded annually during the rains, only small islands of high ground being left above the surface of the water. Wild animals, mainly *sambhur* and hog-deer inhabiting such areas, do not seem to have the sense to leave them before the floods come and become, therefore, marooned on these small pieces of dry land. The neighbouring villagers are quick to take advantage of this fact and sally forth in boats with dahs, spears and dogs, and generally make short work of any animals they find. Many animals are killed in this way every year.

In addition to the illicit methods of killing already mentioned a certain amount of trapping and snaring is always going on, generally practised by jungle villagers with the aid of various primitive and at times most ingenious devices. The amount of damage done in this way is not serious and is in fact negligible when compared with the devastating effects of illicit shooting.

III. Sanctuaries and National Parks.

Most civilised countries have now recognised that no policy of Wild Life Protection can hope to be a permanent success unless it is built on a foundation of secure sanctuaries. Inviolable sanctuaries must be constituted to ensure that a limited number of representatives of every species of an indigenous fauna are perpetuated for all time.

In England there are a number of Game Sanctuaries and additional sanctuaries are continually being constituted. In South Africa and Canada where their national value is perhaps more fully appreciated than anywhere else, sanctuaries occupy thousands of square miles and are visited by over a million people annually. These vast sanctuaries which, besides assisting in the perpetuation of wild life, afford recreation grounds for masses of the population are termed 'National Parks'. People from the cities and large towns flock to them annually in increasing numbers and spend their holidays observing and studying the wild creatures amidst magnificent scenery thus benefiting enormously from the healthy exercise and fresh air.

If only the youth of Burma could be persuaded to divert its attention from the cinemas and less healthy places of amusement in Rangoon and other towns and take a delight in improving its general fitness in a like manner, how very much better it would be for the province as a whole.

In Burma there are at present five areas notified as sanctuaries covering a total area of approximately 400 square miles. This considering the total area of the province and the variety of its fauna is quite inadequate and further areas will have to be notified in the near future if all species are to receive the protection they require.

Burma's existing sanctuaries are as follows:—

Name of sanctuary	Area in Sq. miles	Forest Div. in which situated	Species for which the sanctuary is primarily constituted
Pidaung ...	260	Myitkyina ...	Elephant, Bison, *Saing*, Sambhur, Hog-Deer, *Gyi*, Pig, Tiger, Leopard, Bear.
Shwe-U-Daung.	81	Mogok ...	*Rhinoceros sumatrensis*, Elephant, Bison, *Saing*, Sambhur, Serow, *Gyi*, Pig, Tiger, Leopard, Bear.
Maymyo ...	49	Maymyo ...	*Gyi*, Birds.
Moscos Island.	19	Tavoy ...	Sambhur, *Gyi*, Pig.
Kahilu ...	62	Salween and Thaton	*Rhinoceros sondaicus*.

The above statement shows that of the larger fauna *thamin* and tapir are totally unprovided for and any one at all familiar with local conditions will admit the inadequacy of the provision made for rhinoceros, *saing* and hog-deer.

Of the existing sanctuaries, Pidaung and Shwe-U-Daung should be raised to the status of National Parks; Maymyo can never be much more than a Wild Bird Refuge and the Moscos Islands sanctuary is of very little value.

The Kahilu sanctuary deserves special attention. Constituted in 1928 primarily for the perpetuation of a family of *Rhinoceros sondaicus*, it is supervised by two Karen keepers on monthly salaries of Rs. 50 and Rs. 30 respectively. *Rhinoceros sondaicus* is now the rarest large mammal in the world and this sanctuary probably contains the only known living specimens. The local market value of the animals is certainly not less than Rs. 2,000 each, whilst their scientific value is inestimable.

Recently, as a measure of economy, Government dispensed with the services of one of the keepers and seriously contemplated dispensing with the services of the other. Instead of considering relaxation of protective measures Government would be well advised to maintain stricter control over the sanctuary with a view to ensuring effective protection in future.

The preservation of these few surviving specimens of *Rhinoceros sondaicus* is one of more than provincial interest and the question of the future maintenance of the Kahilu sanctuary is one which might well be referred to the Society for the Preservation of the Fauna of the Empire.

Two more sanctuaries are urgently required in Central Burma for *thamin* and these should, if possible, be so selected as to include *saing* and hog-deer as well. One of the areas chosen might be on the Katha-Shwebo District boundary and the other on the borders of Minbu and Thayetmyo. Both these sanctuaries should be constituted with a view to their being raised eventually to the status of National Parks.

In Lower Burma an area should be taken primarily for tapir and it should also provide for rhinoceros, elephant, bison, sambhur and mouse deer. One of the former habitats of *Rhinoceros sondaicus* near the coast in the Mergui District would probably be most suitable for this purpose.

The adoption of the above proposals would result in Burma possessing six effective sanctuaries, four of which could be raised eventually to the status of National Parks; every species of the indigenous larger fauna would be well provided for and the protection of wild life in the province would be placed on a thoroughly sound foundation.

Sanctuaries, if they are to be effective, must:—

(1) be sufficiently large to allow the animals to live in them the whole year round without having to wander outside;

(2) comprise natural game country possessing abundant food, water and cover;

(3) be undisturbed by timber extraction and other forest works;

(4) be sufficiently accessible to permit of frequent inspection by responsible officers and sportsmen;

(5) be sufficiently inaccessible to prevent the animals from being molested and harassed by villagers and others encroaching upon their boundaries;

(6) be free from grazing rights since domestic cattle in a sanctuary spread disease besides reducing the food supply and disturbing the forest; and

(7) possess security of tenure and not be liable to sudden changes of constitution or control. The present system under which sanctuaries are controlled by officials who are continually being transferred and whose personal idiosyncrasies are often unleavened by any permanent and personal interest in the country is most unsatisfactory.

Those sanctuaries which are suitable for constitution as National Parks should be dedicated to the people of Burma for their benefit, education and enjoyment subject to regulations which would ensure that such Parks were maintained and made use of so as to leave them unimpaired for the enjoyment of future generations.

In South Africa the Kruger National Park is controlled by a National Parks Board of Trustees who are not remunerated for their work which is honorary. The possibility of placing all sanctuaries in Burma under the control of a National Trust composed of gentlemen indigenous to the country should be seriously considered. There are probably many educated Burmese gentlemen and many domiciled Europeans and Anglo-Indians who will respond to this suggestion and willingly accept the trust if the situation is brought to their notice. Equally there are certain men from overseas who would abandon every vestige of racial feeling in a common sporting instinct and would assist the Trust. That the Burmese people would react favourably is certain.

For effectual control a National Trust would require a field officer to inspect the sanctuaries and advise the Trust. The transfer of sanctuaries to the control of a National Trust would naturally be gradual and, at inception, should be subsidised by Government and the services of an officer or officers lent to the Trust. In course of time those sanctuaries which are raised to the status of National Parks should be self-supporting and in the meantime the expenditure upon all sanctuaries should be met from an allotment made by Government from the revenues derived annually from the means to destroy wild life.

For the proper protection of all sanctuaries and the development of those selected as National Parks the whole-time services of a suitable officer, responsible to the Trust alone, would ultimately be required. Bearing in mind that the personnel of the Trust would be indigenous to the Province its field representative should, if possible, be a Burman. It should not be difficult to obtain the services of a Burmese gentleman for this post. There must be some who are keen sportsmen and naturalists and the existing records of the work already done in connection with sanctuaries would be of the greatest assistance to him. The Provincial Honorary Game Warden and a few other keen wild life conservationists would probably be only too glad to act at first in an advisory capacity.

The wisdom of handing over such an interest as wild life protection in sanctuaries and parks to the control of an unofficial and indigenous Trust will be doubted by many; but there appears to be no other reasonable alternative. It must be remembered that the formation of such sanctuaries as there are and practically all that has been done for the credit of Wild Life Protection in Burma has been the work of only a very few enthusiasts whose efforts are now in danger of being nullified by the opposition or indifference of officials who have very little permanent interest in the country. The recent history of Wild Life Protection and the forecast suggests that wholly official control on past lines is likely to lead to a worse condition than is the case at present. The introduction of unofficial and national interest may save the situation; at the worst it can hardly lead to worse conditions than those obtaining. It is worth remembering also that an indigenous Trust could sway public opinion and enlist the support of the ubiquitous and often very influential Burmese priests in a manner outside the scope of the overseas official.

IV. Sport.

From the sportsman's point of view Burma possesses many attractions. There are few Forest Divisions in which fair sport with 'big' and 'small' game cannot be enjoyed whilst in certain selected places the possibilities are excellent.

As the development of the country proceeds and the tenure of all waste land becomes settled the larger fauna must inevitably be forced to take refuge in reserved forests. These State forests are extensive and provided that adequate sanctuaries are constituted on the lines already proposed there is no reason why 'big game' should not be perpetuated to accommodate an almost unlimited number of local and visiting sportsmen without any fear of the stock being seriously depleted.

Since the success of Wild Life Protection in the future will depend very largely upon the education of the jungle Burman it is desirable that sportsmen of the right type should visit the more remote forests periodically and endeavour by precept and example to teach the villager to take more interest in the local fauna and its protection. Nowadays, local officials, however keen they may be on sport and natural history, can seldom spare the time to discuss these matters in the villages and jungle in the way that sportsmen on holiday can afford to do.

Statistics show that the head of 'big game' killed annually under sporting licenses is negligible and hitherto there has been a tendency to discourage outside sportsmen from visiting the Province. Propaganda and advertisement of the country's resources have been neglected until the publication of Mr. Peacock's[1] book there was hardly a modern publication of any real assistance to visiting sportsmen.

The cost to a visitor of one elephant shooting license plus an ordinary Game license is Rs. 450. The fact that a flow of outside sportsmen shooting under a proper system of shooting blocks would not only benefit Wild Life Protection by embarrassing poachers but yield large direct revenues does not seem to have been appreciated. Obviously there would be other attending benefits, not the least being that healthy outside criticism and advice with regard to local protective methods would be forthcoming.

During the period 1927 to 1931 when a Game Warden was in office conditions improved. Visiting sportsmen and naturalists were assisted with advice and information and several expeditions were personally conducted. With the suspension of the post of Game Warden decentralisation in these matters was inevitable. An Honorary Game Warden with no special clerical establishment and heavy Forest Divisional work to attend to cannot devote much time to the assistance of sportsmen and so all progress in this direction has unfortunately been stopped.

V. Kheddah Operations.

The capture and training of Wild Elephants is controlled by a 'Plan of Kheddah Operations for Burma' which has been drawn up for the period 1931-32 to 1939-40. Under this plan certain areas have been closed to operations as elephant sanctuaries, others have been classified as areas in which the extermination of elephants is desirable in the interests of the country's development; the greater

[1] 'A Game Book for Burma and Adjoining Territories' by E. H. Peacock, Deputy Conservator of Forests and Game Warden, Burma (retired). H. F. & G. Witherby, 326, High Holborn, London, W. C. Price 12*s*. 6*d*. net.

part of the province in which wild elephants occur has been divided into a number of kheddah blocks to be worked over in rotation by kheddah licensees.

Prior to the compilation of this plan the control of kheddah operations was decentralised in local district officials, many of whom had but a superficial knowledge of the work and often no time in which to supervise it. This resulted in irregularities, unsystematic work and excessive mortality among the captured elephants. Experience showed that centralisation of control was essential for efficiency and the Plan of Kheddah Operations was drawn up on the assumption that control would be centralised in a Game Warden.

During the short time in which a whole-time Game Warden exercised control, much headway was made. Kheddahs were visited periodically and running records were kept of the work of all licensees. By comparison and a study of the work in different Forest Divisions the Game Warden was able to sum up the resources and capabilities of each licensee. The best men were encouraged and those whose work was consistently unsatisfactory were eliminated in order to make room for new men deserving a trial. The general standard of work was raised and the mortality percentage reduced.

With the suspension of the post of Game Warden progress ceased and control is now once more becoming decentralised in local officers. The Honorary Game Warden cannot supervise Kheddah work in Forest Divisions other than his own; the most he can do is to issue licenses and maintain the records from reports sent to him by Divisional Forest Officers. This arrangement is most unsatisfactory and particularly disheartening to those who have laboured to set kheddah work in Burma upon a sound foundation. Government's accepted policy is to raise the standard of work and to build up a reliable and humane agency for the capture and training of wild elephants. These objects can never be achieved with decentralised control.

VI. Elephant Control.

So long as a stock of wild elephants is maintained in Burma periodic damage to cultivation by herds is bound to occur and individual rogue elephants will, from time to time, cause trouble.

Kheddah operations may do good indirectly by reducing the number of elephants available for doing damage, but they also aggravate the trouble by driving elephants towards cultivation from the more remote forests in which the stockades, to be of any use, must be situated. They also tend to break up herds and scatter individuals and small parties over a wide area.

The present arrangement under which anyone may kill by any means, elephants which are actually damaging crops is open to grave objection. It entails shooting at elephants by night with shot guns and light rifles and wounding elephants in traps. This has the effect of turning otherwise normal animals into rogues which become a menace to human life and are often most difficult to destroy. Similarly the system under which individual rogue elephants may be proclaimed by a Deputy Commissioner is unsatisfactory since it authorises any person to hunt an elephant with any kind of weapon. Great harm results from inexpert and indiscriminate shooting, which is entirely foolish and utterly wrong; nevertheless it must continue until Government removes its excuse by undertaking a properly co-ordinated system of elephant control.

As soon as a satisfactory system of control is in force it will be possible to review the present general exemption given to persons to kill elephants in alleged defence of life and property. It is an established fact that a large percentage of guns which are licensed for crop protection are used for poaching. Many of these guns could be withdrawn provided an efficient system of elephant control was introduced.

Without further delay at least six men should be recruited, trained and kept in readiness to deal with crop raiding and rogue elephants in any part of Burma. These men armed with Government Rifles and working under a set of comprehensive rules should be sent to districts as required. In addition to ordinary crop protective work in the permanent kheddah blocks, these experts would complete the extermination of elephants in those blocks in which extermination is desirable and in which the elephant stock has been reduced to a level at which kheddah operatives can no longer be induced to work. The men should be recruited, trained, paid and controlled by a Provincial Game Warden.

VII. A Wild Life Protection Society.

Attention has been invited to the critical conditions which are affecting the fauna of Burma, the urgent necessity for remedial measures and the ways in which the situation may be improved. Most of the proposals put forward invite action on the part of the local Government, and Government is disinclined to act in matters of this nature in the absence of public opinion. In Burma public opinion in favour of Wild Life Protection is non-existent and until it is created little progress is likely to be made.

Periodically for the last ten years the formation of an Association or Society as an unofficial centre for fostering public opinion in favour of the conservation of the local fauna has been considered. So far nothing has materialised and since the need for such a Society is now greater than ever the sooner the matter is taken up seriously the better.

Ignorance is perhaps the greatest enemy of Wild Life Protection. Ignorance regarding wild animals and birds, their identity, habits, food and utility is general; and people do not care to protect that of which they know nothing.

A provincial Wild Life Protection Society inaugurated by influential nature-lovers and sportsmen, and supported by educated members of all communities, could do an immense amount of good. Such a Society working in collaboration with the Society for the Preservation of the Fauna of the Empire, the Bombay Natural History Society and the Royal Society for the Protection of Birds could, by widening knowledge, evoking sympathy and promoting interest in the local fauna, create and foster a healthy form of public opinion.

The Society should aim at the creation of a public opinion that will demand and support amended legislation for the better protection of the fauna. It should endeavour to gain widespread support from Buddhist priests, teachers, magistrates, property-owners and agriculturists. It should organise educational efforts on the lines of lectures, publications, leaflets and answers to correspondents on questions of food, status, habits. legal protection etc., of wild animals and birds.

A Wild Life Protection Society organised and run as outlined above would give a great impetus to Wild Life Protection and the Province as a whole would benefit enormously from its achievements.

VIII. The Appointment of a Game Warden.

The recent abolition of the post of Game Warden has led to a situation that deserves serious consideration. Financial stringency was no doubt the main reason but failure to appreciate the consequences of that retrograde step was probably the chief cause of the calamity. The urgent necessity for the re-appointment of a whole-time Game Warden has already been stressed and unless action is taken at the earliest opportunity the progress made during the past six years will not be maintained and no further headway will be made with Wild Life Protection in Burma.

The protection and exploitation of the fauna is not the kind of work that can be safely decentralised unless the average executive officer realises that such work is not an optional but a compulsory duty which he must study. Centralisation of the work in a Provincial Game Warden is essential both in the interests of organisation and the education of the executive.

In 1926, in view of the increasing number of firearms and the development of the country the position with regard to Wild Life Protection became serious. A conference was held and it was decided that the appointment of a whole-time Game Warden was essential for the proper protection of the wild fauna.

In 1927 the post of Game Warden was constituted and it was held by a European Forest Officer for three years. At the end of 1931 the post was suspended but the records were maintained by a Forest Officer who was appointed Honorary Game Warden in addition to his normal duties in a Forest Division.

During the period 1926 to 1931 all matters pertaining to the protection and exploitation of the wild fauna, were centralised in the Game Warden. All protective legislation was thoroughly revised, the capture and control of wild elephants were systematised. New sanctuaries were constituted; the reservation of uncultivable land in the interests of the fauna was pushed forward. The question of developing certain sanctuaries in the direction of National Parks was considered, and a growing tendency to treat Wild Life Protection with indifference was corrected. Details of the work done are summarised in the Game Warden's Annual Reports for the years 1929, 1930, 1931 and 1932.

At present, a Forest Officer is appointed Honorary Game Warden in addition to his primary duties as officer in charge of a Forest Division. This is of little use. The honorary appointment carries with it small power to mitigate any but the most flagrant deviations from commonsense practice and the Honorary Game Warden's forest duties leave him with little time in which to deal with protection in divisions other than his own.

IX. Revenue and Expenditure.

It is estimated that the wild fauna, excluding fish, directly or indirectly, produces revenue to the extent of at least, Rs. 1,30,000 per annum.

The sources from which this revenue is derived together with very conservative estimates of the amounts obtainable annually are given below:—

	Rs.
(1) License fees for firearms licenses for sport and for protection against wild animals ...	50,000
(2) Import duties on sporting weapons and ammunition	50,000
(3) Game and kheddah license fees	8,000
(4) Royalty on elephants captured	9,000
(5) Sale of products of wild animals	10,000
(6) Compensation and fines on account of offences against the Game Laws	3,000
Total ...	1,30,000

Trade depression and the general shortage of money may cause a considerable decrease in the revenue obtained from game and kheddah licenses and from the royalty on captured elephants, but, it is doubtful whether the revenues derived from license fees and import duties on account of sporting weapons and cartridges are similarly affected. At present there are probably not less than 20,000 sporting guns and rifles in Burma. All these weapons produce revenue directly or indirectly but although a great deal of money is being obtained from this means of destroying wild life very little is being spent on protection.

Since the Forest Department is responsible for the issue and control of game and kheddah licenses and for the enforcement of protective legislation, a fraction of the establishment charges of that department must be debited to Wild Life Protection. Beyond that, however, all the country is spending annually upon the conservation of a valuable national resource—at present a rapidly disappearing possession—is the sum of approximately Rs. 4,000 which represents the pay of the staffs in the Pidaung and Kahilu Game Sanctuaries.

The constructive proposals now put forward for placing Wild Life Protection in Burma upon a sound foundation entail an annual expenditure of approximately Rs. 50,000 allotted as follows:—

	Rs.
Pay and allowances of a Game Warden ...	20,000
Pay and allowances of a Game Warden's establishment	5,000
Constitution and maintenance of six sanctuaries ...	20,000
Elephant control	5,000
Total ...	50,000

This is considered to be the minimum sum with which any substantial progress with Wild Life Protection can be effected.

X. Conclusion.

Wild Life Protection in Burma is now in a critical state. Factors responsible for the present situation have been discussed and remedial measures have been proposed. Conditions were serious in 1925 but they improved between 1926 and 1931 when a Provincial Game Warden was in office. Now, things are reverting to the state they were in six years ago and prompt action is necessary to prevent irreparable damage from being done.

The lines on which action should be taken have been indicated and the chief constructive acts proposed are tabulated below:—

(1) The re-appointment of a Game Warden with the necessary establishment.

(2) The establishment of a properly co-ordinated system of Elephant Control centralised in a Game Warden.

(3) The centralisation of control of Kheddah Operations in a Game Warden.

(4) The revision of existing legislation and the replacement of the Burma Game Rules, 1927, and the Wild Birds and Animals Protection Act, 1912, by a new Wild Life Protection Act for Burma.

(5) The formation of a Wild Life Protection Society to create a Public Opinion that will demand and support amended legislation.

(6) The constitution of three new Sanctuaries, two primarily for *thamin* and one for tapir.

(7) The transference of control of all Sanctuaries to a National Trust which will develop those suitable for raising to the status of National Parks.

(8) The annual allotment of Rs. 50,000 for expenditure upon Wild Life Protection; the money to be taken from revenue derived from Wild Life Destruction.

'Wild Life Protection' does not mean the 'Artificial Protection' of 'Wild Life'. It means a fight against 'Artificial Destruction'—destruction, that is to say, which is not of Nature's ordering but brought about by ignorance, selfishness, callousness and greed. These are the factors which are destroying the Wild Life Resources of the Province, and which will, if not eliminated, cause the loss of one of Burma's most priceless possessions.

January 10, 1934.

PRINTED AT THE DIOCESAN PRESS, MADRAS—1935. C3568.

THE PRESERVATION OF WILD LIFE IN INDIA.

No. 7. THE MADRAS PRESIDENCY.

BY

R. D. RICHMOND, I.F.S. (*retd.*).

Provisions for the Protection of Wild Life.

In a consideration of the preservation of the fauna of the Madras Presidency it is to be remembered that here, as in the rest of British India, the State owns large areas which have been constituted Reserved Forests and which, *if properly administered* in this regard, form permanent abodes for game and other animals. All possible types of country are represented and all the larger animals, with the exception of the antelopes, are thus provided with *potential* sanctuaries. The habitat of the antelope is for the most part the plains and open fields, but there are certain areas of reserved forest in which they are able to, and do, take refuge.

The area under the control of the Forest Department is some 16,000 sq. miles. Under the Forest Act simple trespass is an offence and shooting is not permitted except on license, the grant of which is governed by close conditions. Game protection *is a definite duty* of the forest staff and even if the charges are large (the average of a divisional charge is over 500 sq. miles of forest and that of a beat, the smallest division is 10 sq. miles) the machinery for protection exists.

Thus the fauna is provided with somewhere to live permanently and an organization to protect it, even if the personnel of that organization is small and sometimes neglectful of this particular item of its duties. But while there can be no chance of the 16,000 sq. miles of Reserved Forest being appreciably reduced there is a danger of comparatively small areas essentially the habitat, or within dangerous proximity of the habitat of particular species e.g. the Nilgiri Tahr and the gaur, being alienated and to guard against this a second line of defence has been devised, such areas being declared to be game preserves. The whole 16,000 sq. miles is of course a game preserve, but the whole of it is not *essential* to the preservation of the fauna and, where certain species would find themselves unduly restricted by the alienation of the country they exist in, special steps have been taken to preserve it as public property. Although any area may at any time be closed permanently, or temporarily, to the shooting of all animals, or any particular animal, the policy is not to form preserves of considerable area, in which nothing may be shot, as it is considered that one of the best methods of controlling poaching lies in the presence of licensed sportsmen. Shooting is closely regulated in theory at least; though a license to cover a year's shooting, except in two areas where the shooting is controlled by specially formed associations, may be obtained for the very small sum of 15 shillings. The number of head of each kind which may be shot is prescribed, as is the size of head, the sitting up over water holes or in machans is forbidden and modern tendencies have been guarded against by the prohibition of shooting from motor cars or with artificial light, except in the case of carnivores. Certain animals other than those preserved for sport and which were becoming scarce e.g. the Malabar squirrel and the black monkey are specially protected, while the shooting of game and other birds is regulated to some extent. Orders exist prohibiting the grazing of cattle in areas specially assigned to the gaur, this step being taken to save them from contact with rinderpest. The grant of rewards for the destruction of wild dogs has been resumed.

While the closest attention is paid to certain classes who will not ordinarily infringe the rules, it is to be feared that the Indian license-holder, few of whom shoot for sports' sake, who pays little attention to the conditions of his license, and who will entrust his gun to other parties, is poorly controlled. And of recent years the policy has been to grant licenses to possess arms to a greater and greater extent, and any one with a gun who lives within reach of areas containing game, is a potential poacher. Also a class of license, that for crop protection, is responsible for considerable damage; damage which might be mitigated would those responsible consent to the peasant being put to the inconvenience of depositing his arm with the police at times when there are no crops to protect. A further handicap to game conservation is the extremely rapid Indianization of the Forest Service: officers of the new class take at present little or no interest in natural history, or in the preservation of wild life and, as a rule, other activities prevent them from paying sufficient attention to a part of their duties with which they are in little personal sympathy. The difficulty is that there is no public opinion on the subject of game preservation in the country and until this has been created, little will be accomplished. The jungleman is principally poacher, for food or to obtain meat for sale.

The Status of Wild Life.

In the Godavari, where the gaur is probably on the increase, chital and sambur are not as numerous as they were: much of the damage, strangely enough, being done with the bow and arrow. For very many years there has been little game in the Ganjam district, so little in fact that the balance of nature is upset and the district is principally notorious for man-eating tigers. The populated north of the vast tract of Vizagapatam and Jeypore, which is a native state, has little game left in it, but the sparsely populated south is well off for all kinds and is the only place in the Madras Presidency where the buffalo is found. Very little of these areas are Reserved forests. The Eastern Ghats are of little interest, except for chinkara at the foothills and some antelope on the plains. The 2,000 sq. miles of the

Nallamalai hills contain plenty of game of all kinds and it is strange that the gaur does not occur. What are known as the Ceded Districts contain very little at the present day. Once the haunt of the elephant, forest destruction preceding cultivation, and accelerated by the goat, has had the inevitable result of driving the game away as well as of reducing parts of the country almost to the condition of desert. There are however, still antelope and chinkara, while sambur are to be found on the hills of Cuddapah and Chittoor; in fact there is still plenty of game in the latter district, even if the glory of the Chamla Valley has departed—due to fewer Europeans visiting it. The Javadi and Salem hills contain gaur which are closely protected and which do some damage to forest works, but the rest of the game animals are poorly represented. The same may be said of the Madura District, principally interesting from the fact that a herd of gaur was cut off when the railway was constructed and, well protected, have persisted. The Palni hills of Madura provide representative animals on the slopes, the Nilgiri goat (*Hemitragus hylocrius*) on the edges of the plateau (7,000 ft.), while the gaur occasionally visits the plateau. But protection is none too good in spite of a constituted game association. Tinnevelly is moderately well off and here too the Nilgiri goat is to be found, though the numbers have decreased considerably. The forest area of South Coimbatore is famous for the 'Grassy Hills', on the borders of the Cochin State, at an elevation of 6,000-8,000 ft.; the Nilgiri goat being common, while elephant and gaur are to be found on the open grass. This forest division contains, in one particular part, the white bison which appears to be developing into a distinct variety.

The North Coimbatore and Kollegal divisions have perhaps suffered more than most, including, as they do, so many villages, from the increase of poaching; but other and perhaps temporary factors are at work, if anything is to be inferred from the varying incidence of the number of game animals in a certain locality. Reported in 1893 as denuded of game, once very common, the old state of affairs was restored from 1901 onwards while there is now again complaint of scarcity. Elephants have increased to an inconvenient extent in numbers of recent years.

The forests of Malabar, that is to say the protected areas, for there are very considerable tracts of private forest land in which there is no protection or shooting regulation, are for the most part exceedingly well stocked with game and other animals of all kinds, particularly elephant and gaur—the forest areas belonging to Government are more compact than elsewhere and there is far less population inside them and on their edges—consequently there is less poaching.

To judge by the complaints of damage done by wild animals it would be supposed that South Kanara teemed with wild life; but such is far from being the case, the complaints being in reinforcement of agitation for the abolition of the forests. But in the upper hills there are sambur and there are a few gaur—also elephants. The tiger, accused of killing great numbers of domesticated cattle (and it is a fact that the mortality of cattle from wild animals is greater here than elsewhere) is in fact rare, the delinquent being the panther, living in low rocky hills distant from the real forests, and killing cattle as there is nothing else to live on.

The Nilgiris, a district at elevations from 1,000-8,000 ft., is richer in fauna of all kinds than any other. Naturally well endowed in this respect, protection in the last forty or fifty years has been good on the whole. The shooting is regulated by a Game Association, the members of which are those who take out annual shooting licenses—these are mostly Europeans—and a special protective staff is entertained. The Nilgiri Tahr, its habitat is the Nilgiris (north of which the family is unrepresented until the tahr is found in the Himalayas), Madura, parts of Malabar, Cochin, Travancore and Tinnevelly in the extreme south, has definitely increased of recent years; sambur abound on the plateau (a beneficial practice is now permitted in the shooting of a limited number of hinds), gaur, vulnerable to epidemics of rinderpest from time to time, chital and sambur are common on the slopes and lower plateau, muntjac are exceedingly common, as are also elephants. Tigers are commonly found on the upper plateau. The extension of the planting industry has reduced the area available, but there is still plenty of room and, whereas certain animals may appear to be reduced in numbers from time to time in different places, there seems to be no ground for apprehension that game animals are decreasing. A falling off in the number of sambur stags shot by license-holders by no means justifies the belief that this deer is becoming more scarce—the fact is that there are fewer warrantable stags to shoot for the reason that the best have been shot year after year.

Recommendations.

There is no need to apprehend that the fauna of Madras is decreasing to a dangerous extent *at present*, though it would be idle to pretend that there are not forces at work which should be guarded against. Apathy on the part of a new class of officer, who is not interested in sport or natural history, and the increased facility with which arms may be legally possessed may both be corrected. Public opinion may in course of time be developed, though this will necessarily be a slow process and it will be fatal if the impression is formed that the interests of the cultivator will not be protected. There is ample room for the wild animals in the considerable areas of forest land which is the property of the state and which need never be alienated, all that is required is the determination to make protection effective. 'Preserves', in this Presidency at all events, appear to be uncalled for—the whole of the forest area is a 'preserve'—and the regulations permit of certain parts being closed to shooting either permanently or temporarily. 'National Parks', if by these are meant areas which are specially protected and in which no shooting by the public is allowed, but which are maintained so that the public may see and study the habits of wild animals, are on a different footing. These should be of great general interest and educational value and tend to promote that public opinion which is so desirable. A difficulty in connection with these 'National Parks', however, is their location; they should be near areas of considerable population, and be served by roads; also the forest should be of a type which allows of the animals being easily seen. It is perhaps sometimes overlooked that conditions in different countries vary and that what may be suitable in Africa, for example, is inappropriate in Madras.

It will not be easy to find an area which fulfils all the essentials; a considerable sum of money will ultimately be required and it cannot be expected that National Parks will be self-supporting; but the first steps are being taken and it may be hoped that they will bear fruit.

Suggestions are from time to time heard as to the desirability of establishing a separate game department under a Warden. Those who advance this view possibly have the conditions of Africa in mind; in India there is already an organisation one of the duties of which is to protect the animals as in the case of the other contents of the forest—the appointment of a Warden, and some additional staff, would lead to dual control and friction: nor is there any need for it. Properly controlled and supported, with some strengthening in certain places, the ordinary staff of the Forest Department *should* be well able to do what is required.

But the Department requires greater support. It is essential that the authority responsible for the issue of licenses under the Arms Act should consult the forest authorities on applications, in respect of residents in, or near, the forest; that guns concerned in shooting offences be confiscated, that the Magistracy should attach greater importance to offences of this class and it is extremely desirable that the sale of flesh at certain seasons should be declared illegal. Finally it is anomalous that the head of the Forest Department should, in theory, be unconcerned with this branch of the work of his department, at present in the hands of an authority which has no occasion to go into the forests and which is not in any way concerned with other branches of forest administration.

COMMENTS ON MR. RICHMOND'S NOTE.

BY

R. C. MORRIS.

In the note on the 'Game Preservation in the Madras Presidency' it is mentioned that there is an area of 16,000 sq. miles providing a natural Sanctuary for the fauna with the Forest Department as an organisation to protect it, the protection of game being a definite duty of the Forest staff.

This may be said to apply to nearly every country holding forests with a Forest Department to control the same. Although in theory the machinery for protection exists, and shooting is regulated, in practice it has been found, and I fear always will be found, that Game Protection is relegated to the background as Forest Officers find that the whole of their time is taken up by other work, in other words the preservation of the fauna takes a back seat to the protection of the flora. That the Forest Department have failed to afford the necessary protection for the fauna cannot be gainsaid, nor can Forest Officers be expected to devote the required amount of time to Game Preservation, however interested they might be in the matter, and I am sorry to say that in many cases these days there is little interest.

It is mentioned that areas denuded of game in 1893 were restored to the old state of affairs from 1901 onwards. I think it would be more correct to have said 'denuded of chital' instead of game. I am fairly sure that the author had before him a note written by a Collector in 1893, and if I remember rightly this only referred to chital in a particular area.

I do not agree with the opinion that there is no cause for apprehension that the fauna of the Madras Presidency is decreasing to a dangerous extent. This statement covers the whole of the fauna and I consider that chital, black buck and chinkara have certainly decreased to a dangerous extent and will be extinct in South India not many years hence unless steps are taken in the matter. The Nilgai in South India have already gone the same way.

I entirely disagree with the opinion that the appointment of a Game Warden and special staff for the control of a National Park, Game Sanctuary for the fauna in the Ordinary Reserves is unnecessary, nor can I see how the present staff of the Forest Department will be in any better position to control the fauna, still less a National Park or Game Sanctuary, than it has been in the past. I cannot see how any friction could arise if the Chief Conservator of Forests controlled both the Forest and Game Departments, the Game Warden if required being a Forest Officer specially seconded for this purpose as was the case in Burma. To my mind it is quite certain that a Game Department would improve matters considerably whether a National Park was established or not, and if any doubt exists on this point a visit to Ceylon might be made to compare the condition of game in areas under the control of the Game Association or Game Department in Ceylon with that in the areas controlled only by the Forest Department.

I do agree with the author in his opinion that the present dual control in connection with shooting licenses should cease. Shooting licenses should be issued by the District Forest Officers (on behalf of the Collectors). Further no arms licenses should be issued by District Magistrates to people living near Reserved or Unreserved forests without the District Forest Officers being consulted in the matter: more important still Magistrates should be made to take a far more serious view of poaching offences and offences under the Arms Act (illegal possession of guns) than they do at present. Punishments meted out to poachers are ridiculous: an inveterate poacher is not worried at all at the prospect of serving two or three months' imprisonment occasionally.

The status of Wild Life in the Madras Presidency may be put shortly as follows:—

1. (*a*) *Within Government Forests.*

In one or two districts, take Ganjam for example, there is little or no game left. In other districts a few species exist thinly scattered, and *in parts* of the districts of Coimbatore, Malabar, Madura and South Kanara game, with the exception of chital and antelope, is still fairly plentiful. The reason is not far to seek. These districts hold areas which *have been* difficult of access to the poacher and here game still holds its own. Chital and antelope live in country that is easily poached and unless early measures are taken chital, black buck and chinkara will be exterminated in South India not very many years hence, just as the Nilgai have been. I say that certain areas 'have been' inaccessible to poachers as with modern guns and cheap electric torches the present day poacher is a far more dangerous enemy to game than he was in the past. Poachers are now penetrating into parts they have never been into before, and it is a certainty that in course of time no part of the jungle will be free from the poachers' activities. Take for example the Billigirirangans. Were it not for the presence of Planters residing on the hills to put a curb on poaching sambhur on the hills would be exterminated. At the northern end of the hills, in the Kollegal Division far from these Estates, very few sambhur are left, most of them have been shot out by the Sholagas who hold guns (some time back 14 guns were seized in one day, but the Sholagas hold just as many now). In the Mysore part of the hills very few sambhur exist although the area is known as the Chamarajnagar Game Sanctuary. What applies here also applies to other districts with the exception of the Nilgiris where the Nilgiri Game Association run a fairly good show. In the more accessible tracts of the Coimbatore, Malabar, Madura and South Kanara districts the status of Wild Life is parlous in the extreme.

The new experimental measure for the compulsory inoculation of village cattle in the Kollegal and North Coimbatore Divisions should keep bison comparatively free from rinderpest, and it is a measure that I should like to see carried out in other districts where biosn occur.

(*b*) *Outside Government Forests.*

Very little game exists, and the remnant is rapidly vanishing.

2. (*a*) *The species of animals for the protection of which there is a special urgency.*

Chital, black buck, chinkara, 4-horned antelope and, in some parts, sambhur.

(*b*) *Animals which do not require vigorous protection but need a modified form of protection.*

Bison only should be placed in this category.

Legislation.

3. *The effectiveness of the laws at present in force in various Provinces which regulate the killing or trapping of Wild Life in Government Forests. Proposals for their improvement where necessary, particularly in regard to the use of motor cars, dazzle light, nets and pits.*

The present laws in force in the Madras Presidency would be very effective if properly enforced. Suggested improvements are:

(1) Considerable moderation in the issue of gun licenses, especially in areas adjacent to reserved or unreserved forests; (2) the necessity of Magistrates consulting District Forest Officers on all applications for arms licenses when the applicants reside within poachable distance of reserved or unreserved forests; (3) the necessity for far more severe and deterrent punishments on offenders convicted under the Forest Laws and the Arms Act; (4) the necessity for District Forest Officers to treat the subject of Game Preservation as one of their most important duties; (5) stricter rules in regard to the use of motor cars for shooting. It is suggested that the Governments concerned should prohibit the shooting of large or small game within 100 to 200 yards of any public road.

There is already a rule against shooting any animals except the carnivores with a torchlight, and I do not think this can be improved upon if enforced properly.

The stricter enforcement of the laws against netting and pitting, both of which are carried on in out-of-the-way parts (instances have been reported recently), and the prohibition of either netting or pitting in *unreserved* forests.

4. *The control of slaughter of Wild Life outside Government Forests.*

This is a more difficult matter, and I am not sure whether Government have any legal right to put forward measures for the control of slaughter in private lands. This is probably a case of educating the landowners on the matter.

5. *Legislation controlling sale of hides, horns, etc.*

In the Madras Presidency I do not think there is any legislation in force at present prohibiting the marketing of flesh, hides and horns of game animals either in close season or out and such legislation should be enacted at a very early date. A law against the export of plumage exists; and legislation prohibiting the marketing of all parts of game animals throughout the year is very necessary.

Under the heading of legislation I should like to see the Indian chevrotain or Mouse Deer added to the list of animals completely protected, and the use of a shot gun (buck shot) on all deer and antelope should be prohibited.

In Coimbatore a slip is now added to all shooting licenses asking the licensees to look for and report to the District Forest Officer of the Division in which they are shooting all cases of poachers' machans on trees, or hides on the ground, over water and salt-licks which they may come across and this should be made one of the clauses in the Rules attached to shooting licenses. If Government could be persuaded to agree to the immediate dismissal of any Forest Guard in whose beat an illicit hide or machan is found the would-be poacher would receive a tremendous knock, as no Forest Guard is going to risk losing his job to help a poacher whatever inducement the latter may offer him.

Administration.

6. (a) *The desirability of definitely laying on the Forest Department the duty of preserving the Fauna and Flora (and not merely trees) in the areas in their charge;* (b) *the desirability of creating a distinct organisation within the Forest Department for the protection of wild animals within Government Forests.*

I consider it is definitely desirable to create a special department, to be controlled by the Chief Conservator of Forests, for the protection of wild animals within Government Reserved and Unreserved Forests. The control of both the Forest and Game Departments by the Chief Conservator of the Province should remove most causes of friction that may otherwise occur between the two Departments, whether the Game Warden is a seconded Forest Officer or not. However much District Forest Officers are encouraged to treat Game Preservation in the proper light this interest is bound to fade again in course of time and will only be kept alive by the existence of a Game Department with which the Forest Officers will have to co-operate in full. The existence of a Game Department is bound to improve matters whether National Parks or Game Sanctuaries are established or not.

7. *The formation of National Parks or in the alternative of strict Nature Reserves where possible, and* 8. *The question of making separate financial provision or the creation of a special fund for carrying out the work of conservation.*

If the formation of a National Park in the Madras Presidency is considered unfeasible, I do not think the necessity for a separate financial provision will arise as a Game Department would presumably be financed under an increased Forest Budget; but for the creation of a National Park or Game Sanctuaries separate financial provision would be required. Two areas do exist in the Madras Presidency which could be turned into National Parks provided communications are improved, and here the value of having the Chief Conservator of Forests as the head of both Departments will be seen, as in one of the areas the improvement of communications will assist considerably in the extraction of forest produce. In this case the term 'National Park' will not be correct as forest work will be carried on in that area, and it would be a Game Sanctuary, but in either category the control of the fauna in this area should fall on a Game Department, and would have to have a special staff in permanent control special funds for financing the work being drawn from the most obvious sources, i.e., the revenue derived from:—

(1) Game licenses;
(2) Licenses and permits for sporting arms;
(3) Import and export licenses for the above arms;
(4) Duty on sporting arms and cartridges;
(5) Licenses to sell or store sporting arms and cartridges;
(6) Fishing licenses;
(7) Fines and penalties for infringement of shooting rules;
(8) Fines imposed for offences connected with poaching etc;
(9) Sales of confiscated and picked up trophies and parts of game animals and birds (both game and protected).

The other area is I consider eminently suitable for the formation of a National Park and should be self-supporting in course of time.

GENERAL.

9. *The position of the Cultivator in relation to Wild Life and the provision which might be made for the protection of human life and property in the neighbourhood of forests from the ravages of wild beasts.*

The damage done by wild beasts, *other than elephants*, is very much exaggerated. Elephants do a lot of damage, in fact unless early measures are taken to deal with the elephant menace it will be, and has been in the last few years, an intolerable hardship on the cultivator whose lands are adjacent to or surrounded by forests in which elephants occur. It is suggested that one of the best methods to meet the elephant problem is the appointment of three or four salaried men to shoot the leading offending bulls at the time crops are being raided. I say 'bulls' as bulls are generally the chief offenders, they play havoc with the crops, either solitaries, in pairs, or as leaders of herds. The experience in Africa has been, on a few of their leaders being shot, elephants soon recognise raiding crops to be an unhealthy pastime. It is only during the harvest season, or for a month before, that the damage from elephant occurs. Ivory from elephants shot would be handed over to Government and should cover the salaries paid out. A strong fence round fields will keep out most of the other animals that matter. The protection of human life hardly comes into the question as regards the cultivated areas of the Madras Presidency, except it be from elephants, and here again the shooting of solitary tuskers has long been advocated being as often as not potential rogues, and nowadays many of them are wounded by the muzzle-loading and cheap breech-loading guns of the Ryots in cultivation. Solitaries which are not necessary for the propagation of the species, generally hard to tame if captured, often frequenting public roads and bridle paths, are a terror to travellers, and sooner or later an accident occurs. I have said 'tuskers' as mucknas are not generally vicious, being usually of a docile temperament.

One of the most important aspects of bird protection should be kept well to the fore: the necessity of showing the cultivator where he does wrong in killing out many of the species of birds found on his land, and for this purpose an ecological bird survey should be made of every province which will prove of immense value in demonstrating the birds that are the friends and the enemies of the cultivator.

10. *Measures to restrict the possession or use of weapons which may be used for poaching.*

A great curb to poaching would be the recall of all guns issued for the purpose of crop protection; immediately harvesting is over, the issue of weapons to applicants must be curtailed: this is very important.

Rewards should be offered, *and paid out promptly*, for information leading to the seizure of illicit guns, *and action taken to recover the weapons immediately information is received.* What frequently happens is this: A Sub-Inspector of Police receives information that an illicit gun is to be found (either in a hut, a grain pit, a hay-stack or more frequently in a watchman's shelter on a tree). Instead of prompt action being taken days elapse before *constables* are sent to recover the weapon and in the meantime it has been removed. To my knowledge this has occurred time and again, the informers get no reward or compensation for their trouble, and so give no further information in regard to any other weapons they may get to know of. The same delay has been experienced over Range Officers taking action when illicit machans and hides are reported, even when instructed to proceed immediately to the spot by their District Forest Officers. A few days are allowed to elapse before action is taken, in the meantime the poachers get wind of the matter and the machans or hides are removed.

A Forest Guard should be immediately dismissed if a poaching case in his beat is not reported by him. It is suggested that a Monegar, Village Munsiff, or Village Headman should be heavily fined if a case of illicit possession of arms is discovered in his village or villages under his jurisdiction. There is not the slightest doubt that every Village Munsiff or Headman knows exactly what arms there are in the village or villages under his jurisdiction, whether licensed or unlicensed.

No. 8. HYDERĀBĀD STATE.

BY

SALIM ALI.

The Hyderābād State occupies an area of about 82,000 sq. miles of the Deccan Plateau. Its north-eastern boundary adjoins the Chanda District of the Central Provinces, renowned among sportsmen of the last century as an ideal game country. Hyderābād State at one time, not so very long ago, provided some of the finest big game shooting—especially tiger—in India, and even at the present day inspite of the penetration and colonization of vast tracts of forest land and the consequent depletion of wild life, there still exist in the Dominions parts which are in no wise inferior to the best that can be found elsewhere within the Indian Empire. Some idea of the abundance of tigers in the last century can be obtained from the fact that the famous shikari Col. Nightingale (who died at Bolarum in 1868) alone killed during his service over 300 tigers, the majority of which were in Hyderābād territory.[1]

Status of Wild Life.

The wild life of Hyderābād is as varied as it is interesting. Tigers are still comparatively numerous in the forests of the Eastern and Western Circles, which also contain some gaur. Leopards and sloth bears are fairly plentiful; sambhur, cheetal, muntjac, four-horned antelope, nilgai, black buck, chinkara, hyaenas, wild dogs, jackals and wild pig are found in suitable localities, while there still remain a few cheetahs or hunting-leopards and wolves. Besides these, porcupines and many other species of smaller mammals are found. A few buffalo are said to occur in the Eturnagaram Range of the Mūlūg Talūka (Warangal District) but their numbers are very small. The shooting of buffalo and gaur has been totally prohibited for some years past, owing to which they have, for the time being, been saved from extinction.

In his *Reminiscences of Sport in India* (published 1885) Major-General E. F. Burton mentions a herd of twelve wild elephants near 'Percall' Lake in 1847, which were said to be descendants of animals that had broken loose in the wars about 200 years previously. In 1866 this herd had increased to fourteen or fifteen individuals. Nothing is known as to what became of them until the 1909 edition of the *Imperial Gazetteer*, which stated that there was one single female still left in those parts. Despite the above, however, Nawab Ḥāmid Yār Jung Bahādūr, the Inspector-General

---

[1] It is of interest to note that since this article was written, the heir-apparent Prince Āzam Jah Bahādūr and party recently (*ca.* May 1935) in the course of 33 days shooting killed 35 tigers, in addition to bears, sambhur and other game in the preserves of Pākhāl, Mūlūg and elsewhere.

of Forests, informs me that no elephants in a wild state have been heard of in Parkal Taluka within the memory of the oldest man living.

Provision for Protection of Wild Life.

Up to the year 1897 or thereabouts, there were apparently no restrictions in Hyderābād against tiger or any other shooting. The present Game Regulations came into force from 28 September 1914. For the purpose of their application, the Dominions are divided into four circles which include both reserved and open forests. They also include Jāgīr and Samastān forests as well as the private Game Preserves or *Shikārgāhs* of His Exalted Highness the Nizām. The Pāigāh Nobles, who have extensive estates (the largest being that of Nawab Moin-ud-dowla Bahādūr which covers an area of 1,287 sq. miles) the owners of Samastāns, and the Jāgīrdārs manage their own forests and are entitled to regulate shooting on their private domains. The rules relating to close seasons, shooting of does and immature animals, and the restriction against shooting buffalo, guar and hunting-leopards are, however, applicable to them. Theoretically speaking, therefore, no shooting can be done in the State without either a license from the Government or a permit from the Pāigāh Nobles, Samastān-owners or Jāgīrdārs concerned.

According to the Game Regulations only one circle is thrown open for shooting each year from 1 March to 31 May and again for ten days at Christmas. For black buck the open season is 1 December to 31 May. Only half the number of districts comprising such circles are open at a time, and shooting areas in these open districts are also defined. Certain areas are thrown open and others closed to tiger shooting from time to time depending upon the increase or decrease of these animals.

Forest Areas.

The most important game forests at present are:

Eastern Circle.

1. Warangal.
2. Khammam.
3. Karimnagar.
4. Nizāmābād.

Western Circle.

1. Asifābād (formerly known as Jangāon).
2. Nīrmal.
3. Mahbūbnagar.

In addition to the above, the forests of Garlāh Jāgīr and Pāloncha Samastān contain big game.

The three principal *Shikārgāhs* of H. E. H. the Nizām are:

1. Pākhāl, situated in the Pākhāl and Mahbūbābād Talūkas of Warangal District and managed by the Forest Department under whom there is a special *Mūntazim* or Warden and a staff of watchers. Area 345.75 sq. miles.

2. Saroonagar, and
3. Alampalli both situated in the Atrāf-e-Balda District and managed by a special establishment under the Sadrūl Mohām, Sarf-e-khās Mūbārak.

The Pākhāl Preserve contains mostly all the big game animals of the State, while the other two which are in open scrub country, have chiefly black buck, hare, partridge and quail.

The *Shikārgāhs* are governed by special rules sanctioned by the Nizām. The Pākhāl *shikārgāh* was abolished some years ago which led to a rapid felling and bringing under cultivation of some of the jungles, with a corresponding diminution of wild life. About four years ago the preserve was re-established. Though for all practical purposes the area is a sanctuary (H. E. H. himself is not keen on shooting, and the two elder princes generally shoot there only about once a year or so) it is doubtful whether with the exception, perhaps, of tiger, the reservation contains as much game as may be expected. The game-watchers that I came across when on ornithological survey work in this part of the country struck me—most of them—as thoroughly inefficient, and information supplied by them, wherever it could be tested, proved unreliable in nine cases out of ten. From my experience of these men (unfortunately the *Mūntazim* himself had died just a few days before my coming to Pākhāl) it is not inconceivable that a good deal of poaching is tolerated by them, either actively or through indifference or neglect. A proper enquiry alone can show if at the present time game is really in any better position here than elsewhere in the State forests, if indeed as much. Col. R. W. Burton informs me that in connection with the visit of a Viceroy in 1902 or thereabouts, Mr. Hankin, the then Inspector-General of Police, and Mr. Biscoe, Conservator of Forests, went through the Pākhāl country on purpose to see what game there was. They told him afterwards that they had seen *no* 'animal', and only one peafowl!

Depletion of Game Animals.

Inspite of the measures promulgated for the protection and preservation of the fauna, which theoretically speaking should give adequate protection to the existing species, Hyderābād unfortunately is no longer the prolific game country it was during the last century, and even during the past thirty years there has been a steady and perceptible diminution. The chief causes of the decline will be analysed later; in the meantime it is interesting to collate the present conditions with whatever little information we can gather concerning the recent past. In the middle of last century the country between Hingoli and Bōkar (Nāndēr District, Western Circle) was famous for tiger and Col. Nightingale shot many of his animals there. In two seasons (March-April) 1897 and 1899, Brigadier-General R. G. Burton of the then Hyderābād Contingent, killed twenty-six tigers in Sirpūr-Tandūr, mostly round Jangāon—the present Āsifābād. On his last visit to this district in 1899 he still found tigers as numerous as ever, and heard fifteen years later that they were just as abundant.

He always thought there was a great breeding-ground of tigers in the stretch of Hyderābād territory south of the Peinganga River in the Bēla and Rājūra talukas of the Sirpūr-Tandūr District and sees no reason why it should not now be as full of tiger as it was thirty-five years ago. Whatever the reason, those conversant with modern conditions in Hyderābād will agree that this is unfortunately not the case. The Ajanta Range all along the Khāndēsh border north of Aurangābād to Kannad was also famous for tiger in the early part of the last century, but now merely harbours occasional stragglers.

There were a few herds of gaur in Sirpūr-Tandūr in the 1890's. One whole herd was reported to have perished from foot-and-mouth disease at Mānikgarh. These animals are now very scarce, and though I often heard of their occurrence, I actually saw only one pair at Utnoor, and from the footmarks I came across in that part of the country they were obviously rare. Inspite, however, of the total prohibition of the killing of these bovines, I came across more persons than one who boastfully claimed to have shot them in recent years!

As regards cheetal, General Burton says: 'In days when cheetal were in vast numbers in the Kinwat (now I think called the Peinganga Reserve) there were scarcely any in adjoining Hyderābād territory across the river. The same with regard to antelope of which there were vast herds in Berār, but few over the Nizām's border.' It appears therefore that the mischief had already made good progress by the time of which General Burton writes.

Jerdon, in the first quarter of the last century, referred to herds of thousands of black buck in the country around Jālna. According to Col. R. W. Burton there were in 1897-1903 black buck and chinkara along the railway line between Secunderābād and Manmād, but fast being wiped out. In 1892 he saw herds of many hundred black buck when marching through the country. In 1903 these herds had dwindled to a dozen to twenty, not more. Though still fairly plentiful in some of the remoter parts of the Mahrattwāda districts, black buck are fast disappearing with the advance of colonisation and increasing facilities of swift transport, coupled with a complete disregard on the part of the man with the gun for age, sex or season. Herds of more than a few individuals are now uncommon, and heads of any decent size difficult to find.

General Burton says that in 1895-1899 there was plenty of feathered game in Hyderābād—Grey and Painted Partridge and Sandgrouse. This is now in a particularly bad way and needs speedy and drastic measures to restore it to anything like its former abundance.

My work in connection with the recent Hyderābād Ornithological Survey (1931-32) took me to many parts of the country once famous for game, and I made a point of investigating as far as possible into the present state of affairs. On the whole, it seemed to me that compared with accounts of even as recently as thirty years ago, the condition is distinctly poor, and this conclusion has since been confirmed by the State Inspector-General of Forests. It is true that tigers are still plentiful in certain portions of the Godāvari Forest Belt, but a rapid diminution in their numbers is inevitable if the present attitude of apathy is persisted in and things allowed to drift as now. Moving about the country as a non-official outsider, I had many opportunities of entering into conversation with people in every walk of life from whom much useful information could be gleaned concerning the subject. Moreover, once their initial suspicion was allayed and they perceived that my interest was chiefly confined to collecting birds, they came out with a good deal more about their exploits with the larger game animals than it would have been possible to extract by direct cross-examination. All I had usually to do was to lead them up to a point and leave them to damn themselves! Even after due allowance for bravado and for shikari's tales, the magnitude of the wanton destruction of life that goes on everywhere, was manifest.

What struck me as curious was that inspite of the formalities and obstacles in the way of getting shooting licenses and the limits of bags, as prescribed under the Regulations,[1] almost every man possessing a gun boasted of the number of tiger, sambhur, cheetal, often gaur and other game he had shot and was still continuing to shoot! The more discoursive ones could, with sufficient encouragement, usually be made to reveal the objectionable methods they employed, which they often did not unmixed with a certain measure of pride in their achievements. In the course of my wanderings in the forest at Nelipāka (in the Pāloncha Samastān), Amrābād, Ūtnoor and elsewhere, I constantly came upon machāns built on trees or pits dug round the edges of swamps or pools in nullah-beds, etc., from whose concealment these relentless gunners slaughtered every animal that came to drink, regardless of the season or whether it was male, female or young. The pity of it is that in many cases this destruction is made possible not only by a passive connivance of the petty officials who have a share in the spoils, but often with their direct abetment. A petty police, revenue or forest official who hears guns popping off almost every night close to his village even in seasons when there are no crops to justify them, can usually be induced to 'keep the peace' if he receives a leg of venison as hush-money. I say this with first-hand knowledge, and it is a fact known well enough to many of the higher officials with whom I had occasion to discuss the question, but who are powerless to put a stop to the practice under prevailing conditions. Sambhur and cheetal are perhaps the worst sufferers, and in areas where they were plentiful as recently as 10 years ago, a marked decline in their numbers is noticeable.

It is sad, but nevertheless true, that some of the greatest offenders are not the ignorant ryot and the village shikari, but directly or indirectly they are people like vakils, officials (usually, but not always, petty!) and well-to-do and so-called educated

---

[1] Clause 21 even says 'no application from non-officials will be entertained' but this I understand is now obsolete.

citizens who should know better. They either do the slaughtering themselves, regardless of Regulations and time of year, or lend out their guns to professional shikaris, or encourage the latter indirectly by commissioning them to procure game for them or by readily buying up whatever is offered for sale at all times of the year.

This indirect sort of abetment is not confined to four-footed game, but applies largely also to game birds such as partridge and quail. While on survey work on the outskirts of Aurangabad town in the second half of April (1932), I came upon a party of professional snarers complete with paraphernalia and decoy birds. Investigation showed that these men had been commissioned to catch bush-quails for a dinner being given the next day by a military 'Burra Saheb' of the British Cantonments! These professional snarers—Pardis and others—are veritable pests, but it is only thus that they are able to carry on their nefarious operations year in, year out, with the result that in many areas feathered game has been reduced to the verge of extinction. In the words of a highly-placed police officer who was also a keen sportsman and Nature-lover and strived at all times to ensure an observance of the Game Regulations, 'The man with the gun does not do half so much damage (to feathered game) as the snarer. He is like a broom, for he sweeps everything before him into his net.'

Principal Reasons for Depletion of Game.

Some of the causes contributory to the rapid and steady depletion of wild life in the Hyderābād State have been hinted at above. Many of them are the same as obtaining in other parts of India, but there are others which are peculiar to the Dominions and the direct outcome of conditions there prevailing. To tabulate them all, they are as follows:

1. Enormous and continued increase of population in the last two decades as shown by the Census Reports of 1921 and 1931.

2. Improvement, extension and opening up of new roads and railway lines (cf. the Kazipet-Belharsha line and others) and the introduction and penetration of motor cars and buses, which combined with (1), are having the effect of throwing open large tracts of country that hitherto provided a refuge to wild life.

3. The facilities provided by (2) in bringing distant game tracts within speedy and comfortable reach of the man with the gun.

I remember that in October 1925, just after the monsoon, it took me three days by bullock-cart to reach Ūtnoor from Nīrmal. There was no road most of the way and the journey had to be done over cart tracks little better than boulder-strewn ravines, and through swollen streams with rocky beds and steep muddy banks in which the wheels sank to the axle-trees. It was an experience not to be repeated in a hurry, however keen a shikari one might be. With the opening up of the Hatnūr-Ūtnoor road, off the main Nīrmal-Ādilābād road, the same journey was performed in 1932 by motor car in about as many hours! As Utnoor lies in the midst of some of the finest shooting country, the effect of this innovation on game can be imagined.

In the exploits of veteran shikaris of the 1890's, like General Burton, one constantly comes across names of places in the State like Jangāon (now Āsifābād) which it took him days of riding or marching to reach, and with an infinite amount of bandobast for his kit. The place is now accessible by rail and bus within a fraction of the time, and with no more bandobast than the purchasing of one's ticket!

4. Shooting from motor cars and buses both by day and by night is a growing menace. The practice has assumed alarming proportions since the Game Regulations were promulgated in 1914, and since it is apparently not contrary to law, it is freely indulged in by all and sundry.

5. The non-existence hitherto of the Arms Act and the easy availability of cheap guns of foreign and local manufacture, and of gunpowder and percussion caps for muzzle-loaders.

6. Indiscriminate poaching and slaughter of game for commercial purposes at all times of the year.

7. Wholesale snaring, netting and trapping of game birds such as partridge and quail, often at all seasons, and the taking of their eggs.

8. Droughts and epidemics.

9. Wild Dogs.

Remedies Suggested.

1, 2, 3. Increase of population, clearance of forest lands, extension of cultivation and of transport facilities are the natural concomitant of progress, and it would be unreasonable to check these, except perhaps (1), for which suggestions are out of place here! No case can be made out for protection of wild life at the expense of human interests. However, a strict observance of the Game Regulations in such areas should be enforced and punishments of a deterrent nature meted out to offenders uniformly, regardless of rank or social position.

4. Shooting from cars and buses, especially by night with the aid of powerful headlights and electric torches, should be made unlawful.

5. The recent introduction of the Arms Act into the State has not been a day too early. The restriction it will impose on the possession of firearms and on the purchase of ammunition, gunpowder and percussion caps should, if properly enforced, have a beneficial effect on wild life in course of time.

6 and 7. It is a fact that most of the poaching—slaughtering and snaring—is done for monetary gain and is encouraged directly or indirectly by people who have no excuse for pleading ignorance of the law. It is an axiom that if there were no receivers of stolen property there would be no thefts committed which, in the main, is unassailable. Therefore, if the promiscuous *purchase* of the meat, hides and horns of game animals (except perhaps of game birds in season under a regulated system) was made illegal,

as well as the *sale* of these articles, the chief incentive to poaching would be eliminated and a great deal of professional poaching would disappear. I suggest that as regards partridge and quail, areas should be set apart in rotation to remain entirely closed to *snaring* and *trapping* at all seasons, until such time as they become sufficiently replenished. The taking of eggs of all game birds should be made punishable.

8. *Droughts* can be remedied to some extent by the provision of reservoirs and by means of canals and channels leading from them. This has already been partly achieved in certain areas, cf. Pākhāl and Nizāmsāgar Lakes, and others. In times of drought, such places tend to draw round them animals from distant parts and, wherever possible, adequate forest land should be set apart near such reservoirs to provide harbourage to wild life at ordinary times, and specially in seasons of water famine.

Epidemics

According to the Inspector-General of Forests, no epidemics among wild animals are reported, and no measures are taken to protect game in the forest against them. That measures are called for, however, is patent; an instance has been given above of a whole herd of bison being exterminated by foot-and-mouth disease near Mānikgarh and the late Mr. E. Ogilvie, a District Superintendent of Police, informed me that some years ago hundreds of animals perished in the Warangal District in a similar epidemic.

Large tracts of game country have been known to be cleared by rinderpest and foot-and-mouth disease contracted from infected cattle left to graze in forests inhabited by wild animals. Measures should be enforced that as soon as the first signs of an outbreak of these epidemics are detected in village cattle, they should be prevented from being let loose in Government forests containing game. One epidemic of this sort, as is well known, will do damage from which it will be difficult for game to regain its position for years afterwards. Often the damage is irreparable, and in many cases the serious diminution, or even complete extinction, of bison and buffalo in certain areas can be traced directly to disease contracted in this way from domestic cattle.

9. *Wild Dogs* do considerable damage to game, and inspite of a recent suggestion that their ravages have been over-estimated, it cannot be denied that measures devised to reduce their numbers in certain other Indian States and Provinces resulted manifestly in a corresponding increase of such animals as sambhur and cheetal which are their favourite prey. It may be a fact that they actually drive away more game than they kill; but it is none the less true that they do considerable slaughter. Moreover, the game thus driven out often suffers heavily in an indirect way by being forcibly exposed to other dangers perhaps just as great, if not greater. It may, for instance, be driven from its forest fastnesses to the neighbourhood of villages and cultivation, where it stands a good chance of falling to the gun of the village shikari or poacher, or in the case of young animals, to his dogs,

When I was at Āsifābād, the surrounding country was overrun by wild dogs, in consequence of which forests said to contain a fair amount of game ordinarily, were bare. I shot a wild dog which was later sent with the shikari to the kutcheri for claiming the prescribed reward. The Tahsildar was wholly unaware of any reward having to be paid! Enquiries of the Inspector-General of Forests elicited that some years ago rewards were paid for killing wild dogs (as per Clause 42 of the Game Regulations) but due to disuse this had become a dead letter and no rewards were now being paid. In my opinion, no case has been made out for the discontinuance of the rewards and the sooner they are reinstated the better.

The existing Game Regulations, with perhaps a few alterations and additions, are sound enough on paper. Their application and enforcement is quite another matter. Mr. Hankin, a former Inspector-General of Police, tried his best during many years, but though a forceful and able officer, it is doubtful if he was able to effect much. Neither have the authorities at the top relaxed their efforts since, but for all practical purposes the position has not improved. In my opinion the immediate way of dealing with the problem as far as the State is concerned, would be to form a small committee comprised of a competent non-official sportsman and naturalist, and Forest, Police and Revenue interests to go into the matter thoroughly and *de novo*, and to investigate the exact present position of wild life from district to district. Having once determined this, and with due regard to the varying conditions, they should be able to devise practicable measures for giving effect to the remedies suggested above and to any others that may seem to them necessary.

There are extensive tracts of forest in the State which might be demarcated and set apart as Wild Life Sanctuaries on the model of the National Parks now in existence in most civilised countries of the West. Three suitable localities suggested by the Inspector-General of Forests for such reservation are: (1) along the cart track from Āsifābād to Ūtnoor-Ādilābād District; (2) Amrābād-Mahbūbnagar District; (3) around the newly constructed Nizāmsāgar Lake—Mēdak District. For the administration of these reservations and also for a proper administration of the Game Regulations in other State forests, the need of creating a separate and efficient Game Department becomes imperative. This should consist of a Game Warden with a staff of assistants, and watchers of the right type. It should either be subject to the Inspector-General of Forests and work in full co-operation with his department, or better still be directed by a small committee consisting of the Inspector-General of Forests, the Inspector-General of Police, the Revenue Member and the Game Warden (*ex-officio*). By a curious anachronism, shooting licenses are at present issued by the Political Department. Whatever may have been the origin and desirability of this practice in the past, it is clear that the function should now be transferred to the Forest Department where it rightly belongs. Later it could be taken over by the Game Department. The present procedure has little to recommend it; it results in unnecessary inconvenience and lack of co-ordination which does not make for efficiency.

After a proper investigation into the problem of wild life conservation in the Nizām's Dominions, as elsewhere, it emerges more clearly than ever that at the back of all the senseless slaughter and law-breaking, which has brought about the present sorry plight, is the apathy of public opinion towards the need for the preservation of our fauna. The backing of public opinion is vital to the success of a campaign of this nature. Lectures and the exhibition of suitable cinema films should be organised in order to rouse the public from its apathy and make it realise the value and importance of wild life, and appreciate the measures and the arguments put forward for its protection and preservation. A beginning must also be made with children in the schools, by means of properly arranged Nature Study programmes, so that they will grow up to a love of Nature and to a sense of their responsibility for the conservation of wild life which is their natural heritage. Let us hope it will not be too late before the necessary steps are taken by the authorities.

I am indebted for much interesting information concerning game in the Hyderābād State in the recent past to the two veteran sportsmen brothers Brigadier-General R. G. and Col. R. W. Burton, and to Nawāb Hāmid Yār Jung Bahādūr, the State Inspector-General of Forests, for his ready and willing co-operation in supplying me with a great deal of authentic data relating to modern conditions and to the existing Game Regulations and their administration in the Dominions.

DEHRA DUN,

30th September, 1933.

No. 9. MYSORE.

BY

Major E. G. PHYTHIAN-ADAMS, F.Z.S.

The State of Mysore is an elevated table-land varying in altitude for the most part from 2,500 to 3,000 ft. above sea-level. The Western Ghats rising to some 5,000 ft. bound it on the west and break the force of the South-West Monsoon. On the south are the Nilgiri Hills and on the south-east the Billigirirangans, the highest point of which is about 5,000 ft. above sea-level. In the interior the country is undulating and in many parts hilly. Generally speaking the northern part of the State consists of open plains with occasional rocky hills, the centre is the most intensely cultivated, while on the western and southern fringes are the denser forests. The total area of the State is some 30,000 sq. miles of which forests cover over one-tenth. The forests are divided into: (1) Game Preserves which are closed to all shooting and fishing except by special permission; (2) State forests corresponding to Reserved forests in British India where the pursuit of game is illegal except on licence; and (3) District forests which now hold little but small game, panthers and wild pig.

Mysore is the fortunate possessor of a fauna so diverse and varied that few other parts of India can equal it. The extensive open plains of the north are the home of numerous herds of black buck, which extend more or less over all cultivated areas of the State; the more broken country holds chinkara and wolves, while nilgai though uncommon are still reported to exist in certain parts. The forests contain herds of elephant and bison, and a good head of sambhur and spotted deer, while lesser fry, barking deer, wild pig, etc. are common in suitable localities. The State contains some famous tiger grounds and panthers are ubiquitous, though hunting leopards are probably now extinct. Bears are fairly common in certain parts and wild dogs even more so. The list of indigenous small game includes the Great Indian Bustard, Florican, Peafowl, Jungle and Spurfowl, Partridge, Sandgrouse (two or more varieties), several species of Quail, Green, Bluerock and Imperial Pigeons, and the Indian Hare, to which must be added in the cold weather countless numbers of Snipe, Duck and Teal and some Bar-headed Geese, which find rich subsistence in the paddy fields and on the irrigation tanks with which the State is so well provided. Apart from game birds Mysore is particularly rich in bird life both resident and migrant, and it is to be hoped that before long a regular scientific survey of it will be carried out as has been already done in other parts of South India.

The principal rivers of the State are the Cauvery and Kabbany, and on the northern border the Tungabhadra, and there are numerous subsidiary streams, all of them holding the snub-nosed crocodile and immense numbers of fish: mahseer, carp, murrel, labeo, etc. providing not only excellent sport but also an important item of food supply to the population.

The above short survey will show how varied the Fauna is, and it now remains to compare the past with the present, to consider the Game Laws, and to make any suggestions for further safeguarding an asset of such importance.

For information about wild life in the State in years gone by we are largely dependent on the well-known works of Sanderson and other sportsmen. In those days there were apparently no game preserves and one gathers, no game laws either. Big and small game of all kinds was plentiful and the bags obtained were certainly larger than would be possible now. But already by 1900 a distinct decrease was noticeable for Russell writing in that year remarks that: 'One has only to read old sporting books and even so comparatively recent a one as Mr. Sanderson's and to know the forests as they are at this day, to fully appreciate the terrible rate at which game has decreased and is ever decreasing in Mysore'; and personal enquiries from older residents in the State confirm a great decrease of big game in the District forests, and to a lesser degree in the State forests, though the position in the Game Preserves is less unfavourable.

Due consideration must however be given to the inevitable restrictions imposed on wild life by the opening up of fresh areas to cultivation, the increase of population and consequent increased number of arms licences, and improved communications and means of transport, and if all these are taken into account, it would be unreasonable to consider the present position as unsatisfactory, though certain steps are most desirable to prevent further deterioration.

Elephants which are strictly protected as in British India continue to provide sufficient numbers for the famous kheddahs as and when required. There is no dearth of bison and good heads are still obtainable. Sambhur and spotted deer are still to be found in fair numbers. Black buck which in some parts were certainly in danger of extermination before the War have now largely recovered, thanks to protection. Tigers are as numerous as ever in Shimoga and Bandipur though they appear to have deserted Sanderson's old shooting grounds on the south-eastern border, probably owing to all the deer there having been killed off. Panthers continue to be as much a pest as ever. Wild dogs are certainly not on the decrease in spite of the reward placed on their destruction. Bears seem to have changed their habits to some extent and to have become more nocturnal than in Sanderson's time, but though harder to find they certainly exist in fair numbers. Wolves certainly have decreased, which will not be regretted by sheep owners whose herds used to suffer severely from their depredations. Up to about 1914 a few were shot almost every year close to the capital but a careful search in recent years has failed to discover their existence within many miles of the city. Turning to birds the only resident which has seriously decreased is the Great Indian Bustard. A few pairs still exist in favoured localities in the centre of the State, their numbers slightly increasing as one goes north, but at the best there are very few left and their survival if left longer without protection is most unlikely. Great numbers of partridges and junglefowl are snared and sold in the towns throughout the year and this unrestricted slaughter is already having its effect though there is little fear of their extermination at present. Of the migratory birds duck and teal have certainly greatly decreased in numbers during the past ten years but this is a matter hardly within the control of the State authorities though some improvement might be effected in the case of the spotbill duck and whistling teal numbers of which stay to breed locally, were the trade in their eggs made illicit. The shooting of Demoiselle cranes might well be prohibited in certain areas where their pursuit offends the religious prejudices of the inhabitants. Their numbers are so vast that there is little fear of their being seriously reduced, but protection seems desirable for the reason given, as more than one fracas has already occurred in this connection.

So far as is known the only attempt to introduce exotic fauna was the importation of a herd of fallow deer a few years back, but unfortunately the experiment failed as they were quickly killed off by wild dogs There should however be less difficulty in introducing gooral which could be obtained without much trouble from the lower Himalayas and for which an ideal locality could be found in the isolated Gopalswamibetta hill. Such an addition to the fauna would be of great interest as at present this species is unknown in South India.

The Game Laws of the State were revised in 1931 and on paper serve as a model of their kind. In general they follow those in force in the Nilgiris and other parts of British India, but there are two important clauses which strike a new note in Game Preservation in India, viz.: (1) classification of tigers as 'game' with an annual bag limit of two; and (2) imposing on private owners the necessity for taking out a licence before they can shoot game on their own land. The damage done by tigers is often much exaggerated and the help which they give to the ryot by destroying deer and pig forgotten, and the Mysore Government deserves great credit for its bold step in giving them some form of protection, an example which might well be followed in other parts of India. The clause regarding private lands is of course on the lines in force in Great Britain and as such is a distinct advance, though it might have made clear the inalienable right of the owner to game on private land, a most important point which seems to have been overlooked in other parts of India also, as the private owner can do so much to protect the wild life on his land if educated to do so.

A noticeable omission from the Laws is any clause dealing with that modern pest the motor car shooter. Shooting from cars is indefensible; it is not sport but slaughter, and far too many animals escape to die a lingering death. It has been very rightly banned in East Africa with severe penalties, and recently we understand in the Bombay Presidency and in the Nilgiris, and

Mysore which justly prides itself on being an advanced State would do well to follow this good example. At present the practice is on the increase, and one hears almost incredible stories of bursts of rapid fire at herds of bison, of animals shot and left to rot by the roadside, and of lorries specially equipped with spotlights for poaching sambhur etc. at night. No shooting should be permitted within 100 yards of a car, and heavy penalties enforced for breach of this rule.

As has been said above, the existing Game Laws are a model of their kind, but as has been found in other parts of India, it is one thing to pass a law and quite another to enforce it. The public generally and many even of the subordinate officials appear to have no knowledge of the existence of these laws, far less of their provisions, and poaching is widespread and largely unchecked. Public opinion is not yet sufficiently educated to realise the importance of the preservation of the fauna, and until the scope and purpose of the Game Laws are more widely known, it cannot be expected that their provisions will be generally observed. Much good would be effected if the subordinate Government officials of all Departments concerned were made to realise their responsibility in the matter, and this applies with particular force to the Forest Range Officers who if they like can put a definite stop to all poaching.

But still more important is the education of public opinion which can best be effected by propaganda in the Press, by lectures and nature classes in schools and colleges, by the formation of local associations for the study and protection of wild life, and by collaboration with similar societies already existing in other parts of India.

Equally important is the creation of a Wild Life Fund to which would be credited all revenue from arms licences, shooting and fishing licence fees, fines for offences, etc. while the Fund would be used to pay rewards for the destruction of vermin, for preventing poaching, and for the upkeep of a Game Warden and National Park. At present there are in the State no sanctuaries for wild life, though to a certain extent the Game Preserves take their place, but a stricter supervision is required if these are to fulfil a really useful purpose. It is suggested that part of the Bandipur Game Preserve might with advantage be turned into a National Park. This area holds a good head of game and wild life generally, and being adjacent to the strictly preserved Mudumalai forest under control of the N.G.A. could be easily policed. Bandipur lies on the main road some 50 miles equidistant from Ootacamund and Mysore City, and a well organised Park there should prove a great attraction. The existing Travellers' Bungalow could be easily enlarged to provide the necessary accommodation.

There is no doubt that the presence of sportsmen in shooting areas is one of the greatest curbs on the activities of the poacher, and more encouragement should be given them by reducing licence fees which are at present excessive in comparison with the bag obtainable and by throwing open to the general public some at any rate of the Game Preserves.

Legislation is also required to prevent the sale of game in the close season; this would considerably restrict the activities of the motor poacher who shoots solely for gain.

To sum up, the present position of wild life in Mysore is, considering all the factors involved, not unsatisfactory; but this position will certainly deteriorate seriously in the near future unless steps are taken to prevent it, in which connection the following are suggested as most important:

(1) Strict enforcement of the existing Game Laws;
(2) Education of public opinion in every possible way;
(3) Formation of a Wild Life Fund;
(4) Prohibition of all motor car shooting;
(5) Prohibition of sale of game out of season and control of traffic in hides and horns;
(6) Protection for the Great Indian Bustard;
(7) Encouragement of genuine sportsmen; and
(8) Establishment of a National Park.

Mysore has been blessed by Nature with an unusually rich fauna, and every possible step should be taken in time to safeguard it and to make its people realise the importance from every point of view of such a national asset.

By courtesy of *R. B. Holmes & Co.*

Himalayan scenery above tree line.

By courtesy of *R. B. Holmes & Co.*

Himalayan scenery at the edge of the tree line.

Sind : Typical desert vegetation.

Photos by C. McCann.

Rajputana : Semi-desert vegetation.

Photo by C. McCann.

United Provinces : Open deciduous forest.

Photo by Salim A. Ali.

Deccan Trap country : Typical vegetation and scenery.

Assam : Dense evergreen forest.

Photos by C. McCann.

Assam : Interior of dense evergreen forest.

Prince of Wales' Museum, Bombay.

The Gaur or Indian Bison (*Bibos gaurus*, H. Smith).

By courtesy of The Amer. Mus. Nat. Hist., New York.

By courtesy of *The Field Museum, Chicago*

The Wild Buffalo (*Bubalus bubalis*, L.).

By courtesy of The Field Museum, Chicago.

Marco Polo's Sheep (*Ovis ammon poli*, Blyth).

Photo by W. S. Berridge.

The Bharal or Blue Wild Sheep *Pseudois nahoor*, Hodgs).

By courtesy of *The Field Museum, Chicago.*

The Tien Shan Ibex (*Capra sibirica almasyi*, Lorenz)

The Sind Wild Goat (*Capra bircus blythi*, Hume).

The Pir Pinjal Markhor (*Capra falconeri cashmiriensis*, Lyd.).

Photo by F. W. Bond.

The Himalayan Thar (*Hemitragus jemlaicus* H. Smith).

(*Height at shoulder 36-40 in.*).

Photo by *Salem A. Ali.*

The Nilgiri Thar (*Hemitragus hylocrius* Blyth).

(*Height at shoulder 39-42 in.*).

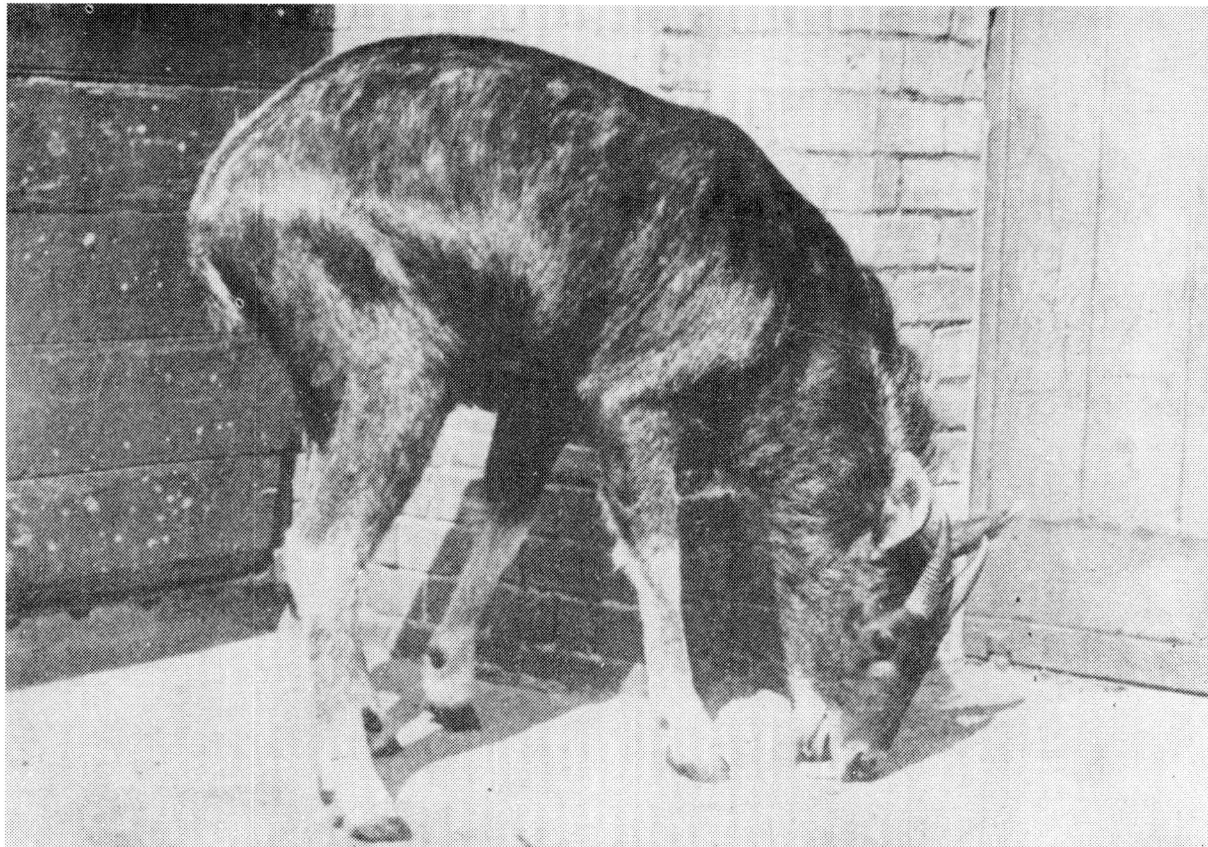

Serow or Goat-Antelope (*Capricornis sumatraensis* Pocock).

(*Height at shoulder 36-38 in.*)

(Height at shoulder: bull 51, cow 42 in.).

By courtesy of *The Amer. Mus. Nat. Hist., New York.*

The Black Buck (*Antilope cervicapra*, L.).

Photo by W. S. Berridge.

By courtesy of *Amer. Mus. Nat. Hist., New York.*

The Sambar or Rusa Deer (*Rusa unicolor* Kerr.)

(*Height at shoulder 5 ft.*).

By courtesy of The Amer. Mus. Nat. Hist., New York.

Swamp Deer (*Rucervus duvaucelli* Cuv.).

(*Height at shoulder 54 in.*).

By courtesy of *The Amer. Mus. Nat. Hist., New York.*

The Brow-antlered Deer or Thamin (*Rucervus eldi* McClell.).

(*Height at shoulder nearly 4 ft.*).

The Kashmir Stag or Hangul (*Cervus cashmiriensis* Falc.).

(*Height at shoulder 48-50 in.*).

Photo by F. W. Champion.

Reproduced from "The Jungle in Sunlight and Shadow." Copyright, F. W. Champion.

The Indian Wild Boar (*Sus cristatus* Wagner).

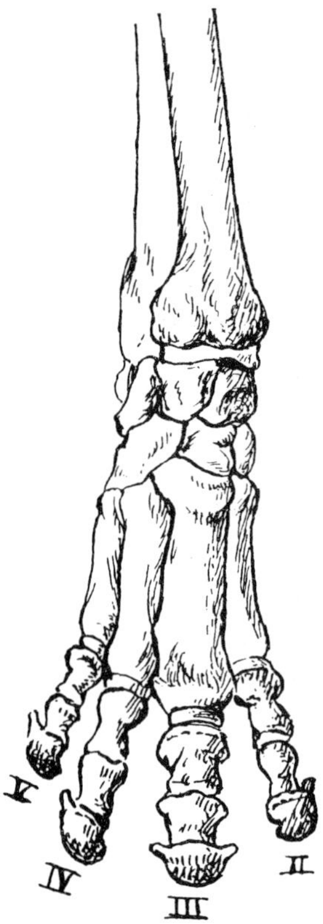

TAPIR.

RHINOCEROS.

HORSE.

The bones of the forefoot of the three animals are shown: the Horse with 1 digit, the Rhinoceros with 3 and the Tapir with 4. In all of them the 3rd or middle digit is symmetrical in itself and much more developed than the other digits.

Photo by C. McCann

The Indian Wild Ass (*Equus onager indicus*, Pallas).
Height at shoulder 44-48 in.).

RHINOCEROSES LIVING: (*facing left*); EXTINCT (*facing right*).

The Baluchithere, an aberrant form of Rhinoceros, whose remains were discovered in the Butgi Hills, Eastern Baluchistan is believed to have been 13 ft. high at the withers. It towers above all its relatives. (*Reproduced from Natural History, Vol. XXIII, No. 3*).

By Courtes of *The Field Museum, Chicago*

The Great One-horned Rhinoceros (*Rhinoceros unicornis* L.).
(*Height at shoulder 60-69 in.*).

By Courtesy o *The Brit Mus Nat. Hist.*).

The Smaller One-horned Rhinoceros (*Rhinoceros sondaicus* Cuv.)

(*Height at shoulder 70 in.*).

By Courtesy of *The Amer. Mus. Nat. Hist., New York.*

The Sumatran Two-horned Rhinoceros (*Rhinoceros sumatrensis* Cuv.).
(*Height at shoulder about 52 in.*).

Photo by W. S. Berridge.

The Malay Tapir and young (*Tapirus indicus* Cuv.).

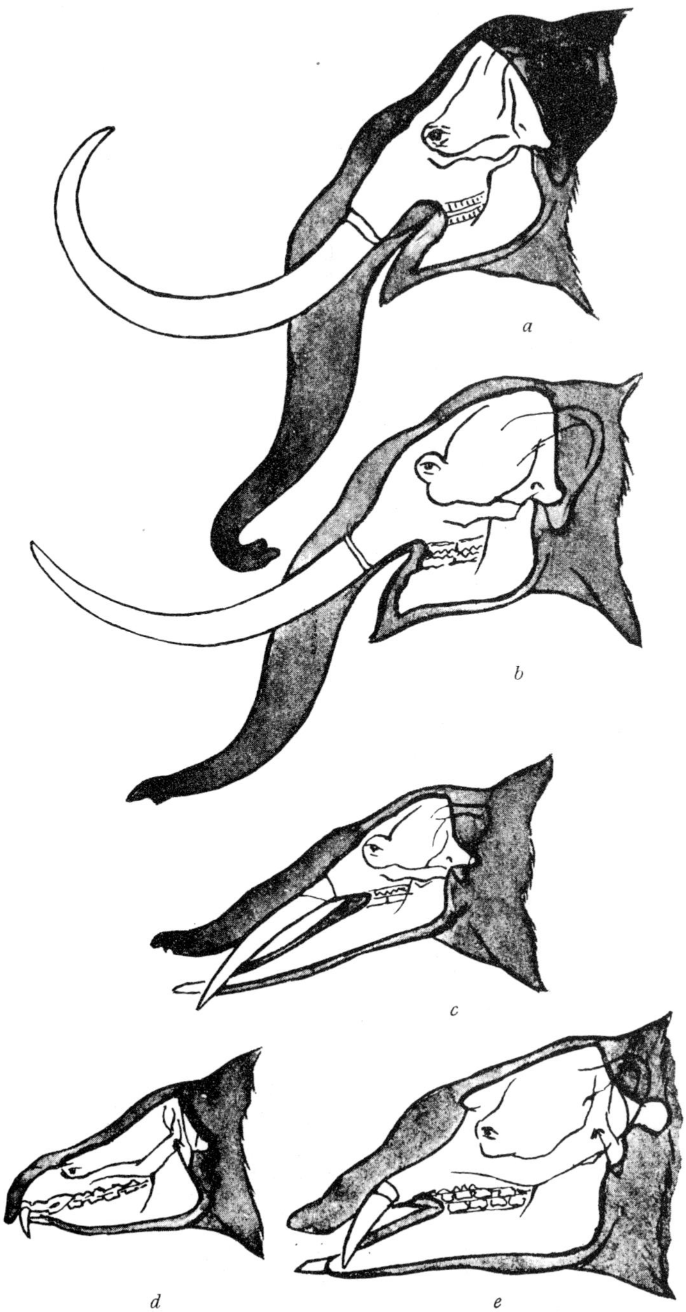

Evolutionary changes of Proboscidea. Based on restorations modelled by R. S. Lull.

a. *Elephas columbi ;* b. *Mammut americanum ;*
c. *Tetrabelodon angustidens ;* d. *Moeritherium ;*
e. *Palaeomastodon.* (*Reproduced from Ann. Report, Smithsonian Institution, 1909*).

Photo by W. S. Thom.

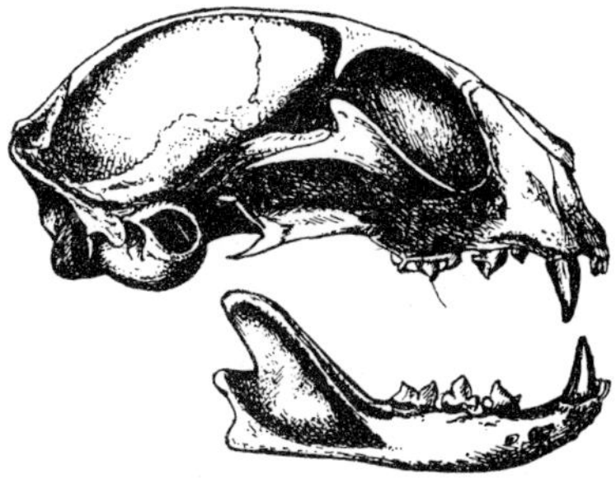

Domestic Cat.

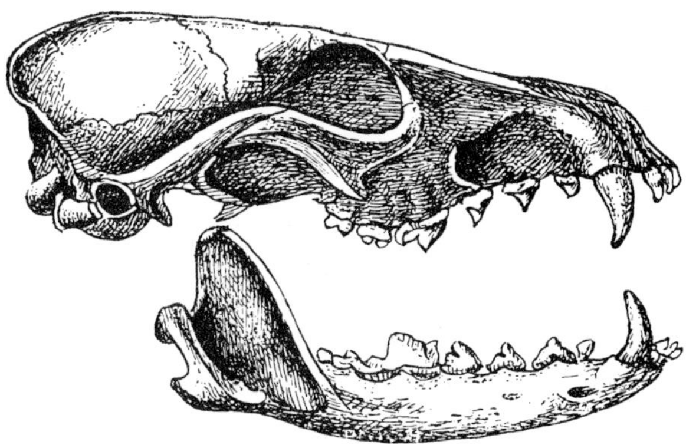

Common Fox.

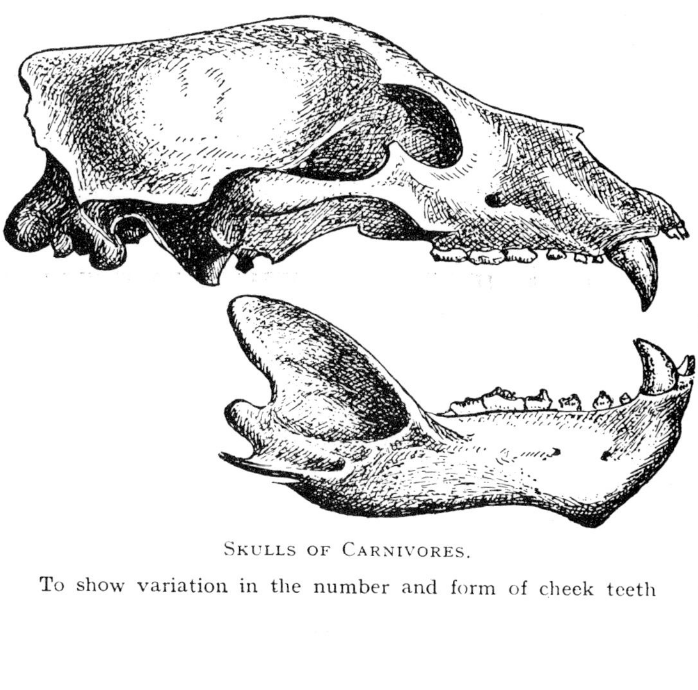

Sloth Bear.

SKULLS OF CARNIVORES.

To show variation in the number and form of cheek teeth

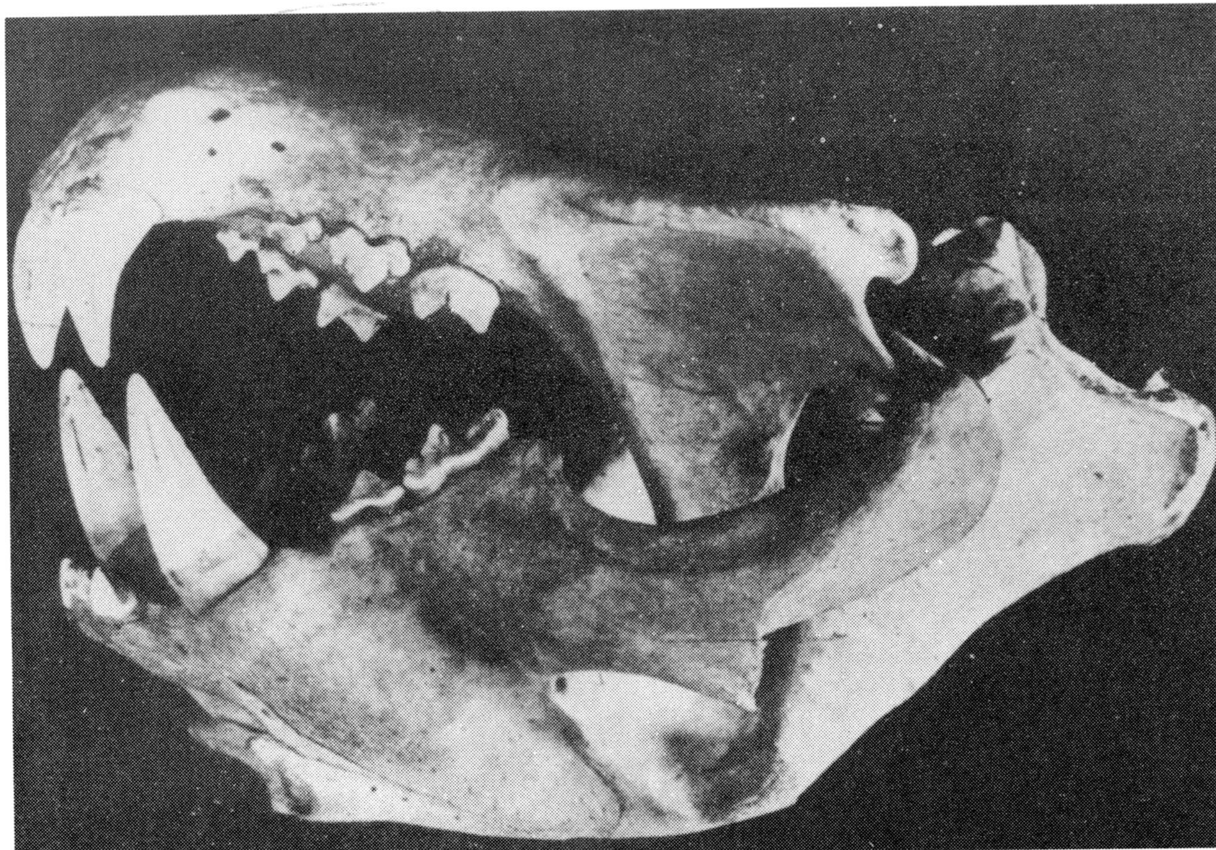

SKULL OF A TIGER.

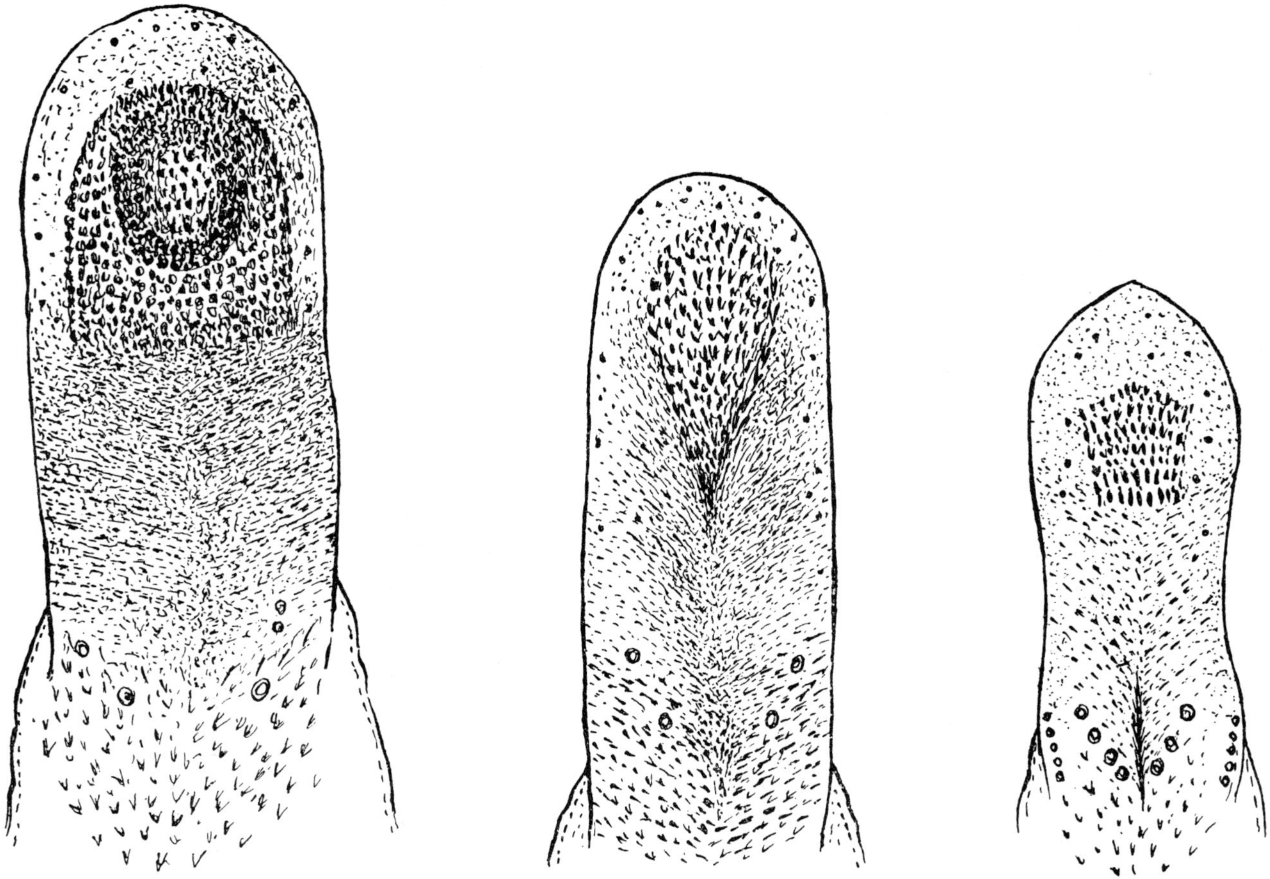

Tiger (*Pantherinae*). Cheetah (*Acinonychinae*). Caracal (*Felinae*).

The sharp-pointed conical papillae tend to form a "spinous patch" on the fore part of the tongue. The proximity of this patch to the apex of the tongue, its posterior limits, the shape of the spines are distinctive on the 3 subfamilies in which the Cat tribe is divided. (Dr. C. F. Sontag, P.Z.S, 1923).

Photo by F. W. Bond.

The Asiatic Lion (*Panthera leo persica* Meyer).

Copyright. F. W. Champion.

The Tiger (*Panthera tigris*, Linn.).

A Tigress feeding on her "kill".

E. H. Peacock.

A TIGRESS AT HER "KILL"

E. H. Peacock.

 F. W. Champion.

The Indian Panther (*Panthera pardus fusca*, Meyer).

Photo by F. W. Bond.

The Snow Leopard (*Uncia uncia*, Schreber).

Photo by *F. W. Bond.*

The Cheetah or Hunting Leopard (*Acinonyx jubatus*, Erxleben).

PLATE XLVII.

Copyright. *F. W. Champion.*

PLATE XLVIII.

Photo by *W. S. Berridge.*

The Caracal (*Lynx caracal*, Güldenstadt).

Pallas's Cat (*Trichaelurus manul*, Pall.)

PLATE L.

del. O. F. Tassart.

The Marbled Cat (*Pardofelis marmorata*, Martin).

The Golden Cat (*Profelis temmincki* Vig.)

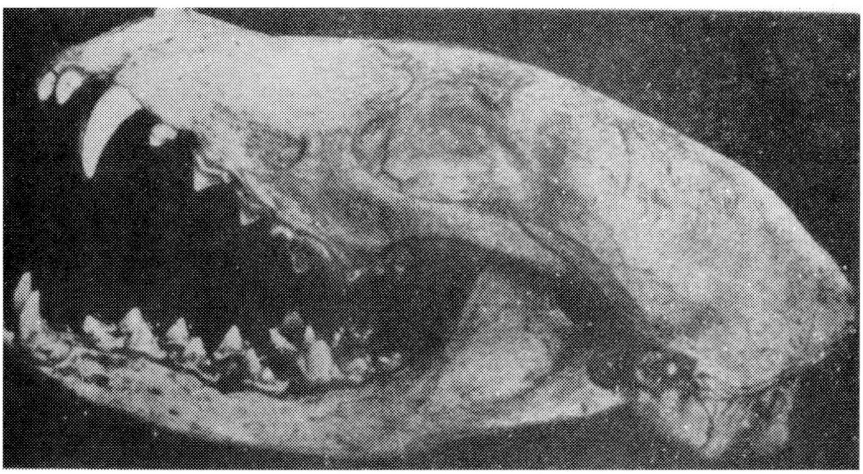

Skull of the Large Civet (*Viverra zibetha* Linn.).

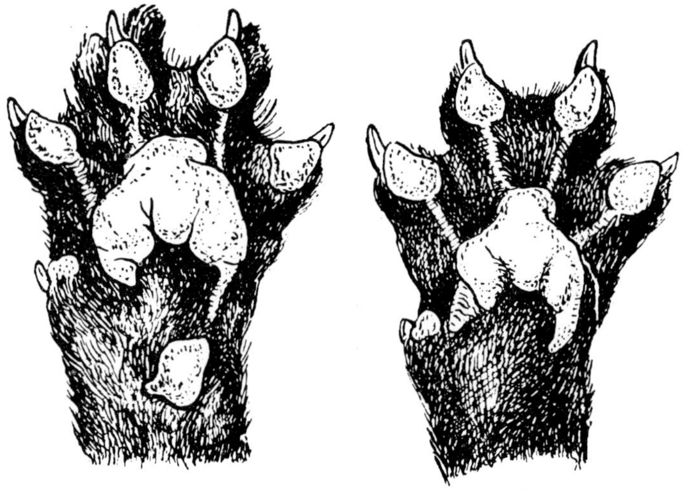

A B

Fig. 1.—Feet of *Viverra zibetha*, a true civet of terrestrial habits, showing hairy soles and reduction of pads. (A, Left forefoot; B, Left hindfoot.)

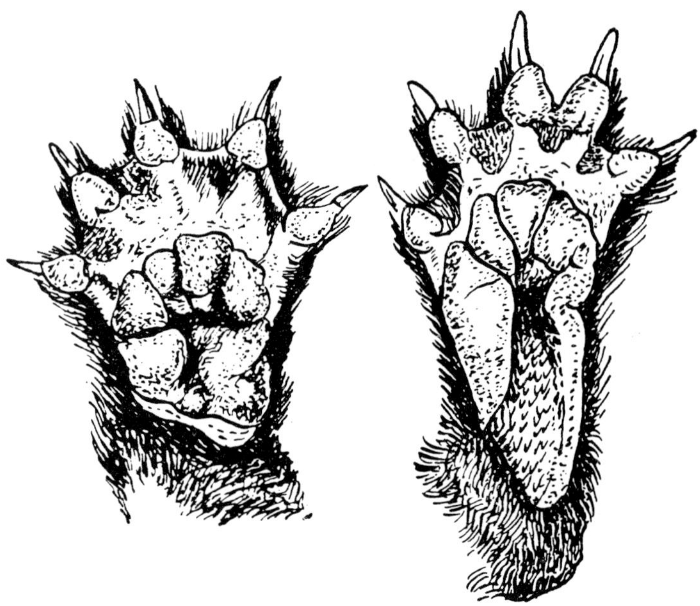

A B

Fig. 2.—Feet of *Paguma larvata*, one of the arboreal Palm Civets showing comparatively naked soles and greater development of the pads for grasping the branches of trees. (A, Left forefoot; B, Left hindfoot.)

After Pocock (*Proc. Zool. Soc. Lond.*).

Photo by *W. S. Berridge.*

The Large Indian Civet (*Viverra zibetha* Linn.).

PLATE LVI.

Del.

The Small Indian Civet (*Viverricula indica* Geoffroy).

PERFUME AND ANAL GLANDS OF CIVETS.

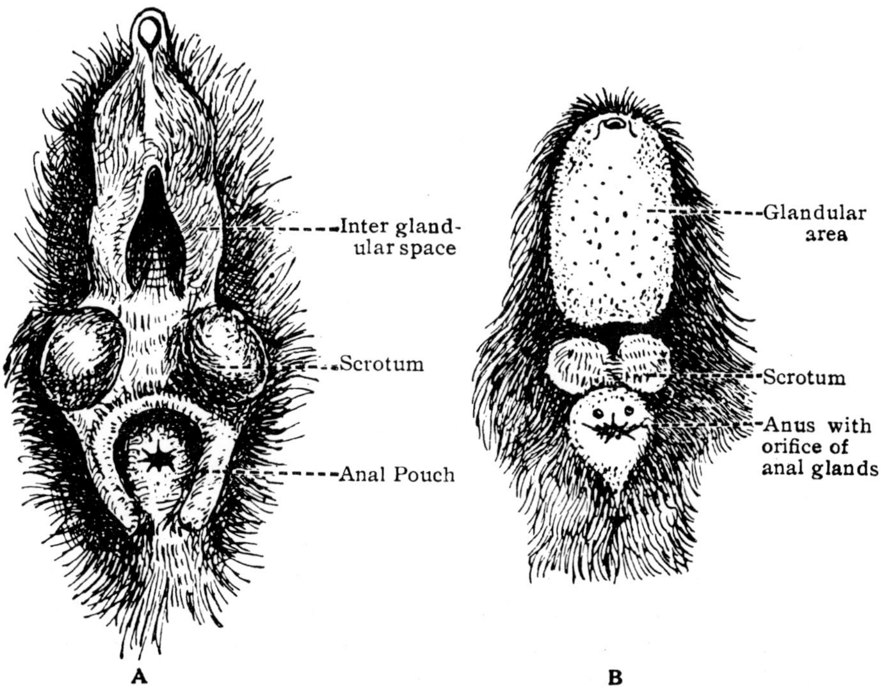

A.—Inferior view of the anal glandular area of the Large Civet *Viverra zibetha* (male).

B.—Inferior view of anal glandular area of the Common Palm Civet *Paradoxurus hermaphroditus* (male).

After Pocock (*Proc. Zool. Soc. Lond.*).

Photo by *W. S. Berridge.*

The Common Palm Civet (*Paradoxurus hermaphroditus* Gray).

The Chinese Palm Civet (*Paguma larvata* Gray).

Photo by *F. W. Bond.*

The Binturong or Bear Cat (*Arctitis binturong* Raffles).

The Spotted Tiger Civet (*Prionodon pardicolor* Hodgson).

The White-eared Palm Civet.
Arctogalidia leucotis Blyth.

The Common Mungoose (*Herpestes edwardsi* Geoff.).

The Small Indian Mungoose (*Herpestes auropunctatus* Hodgs.).

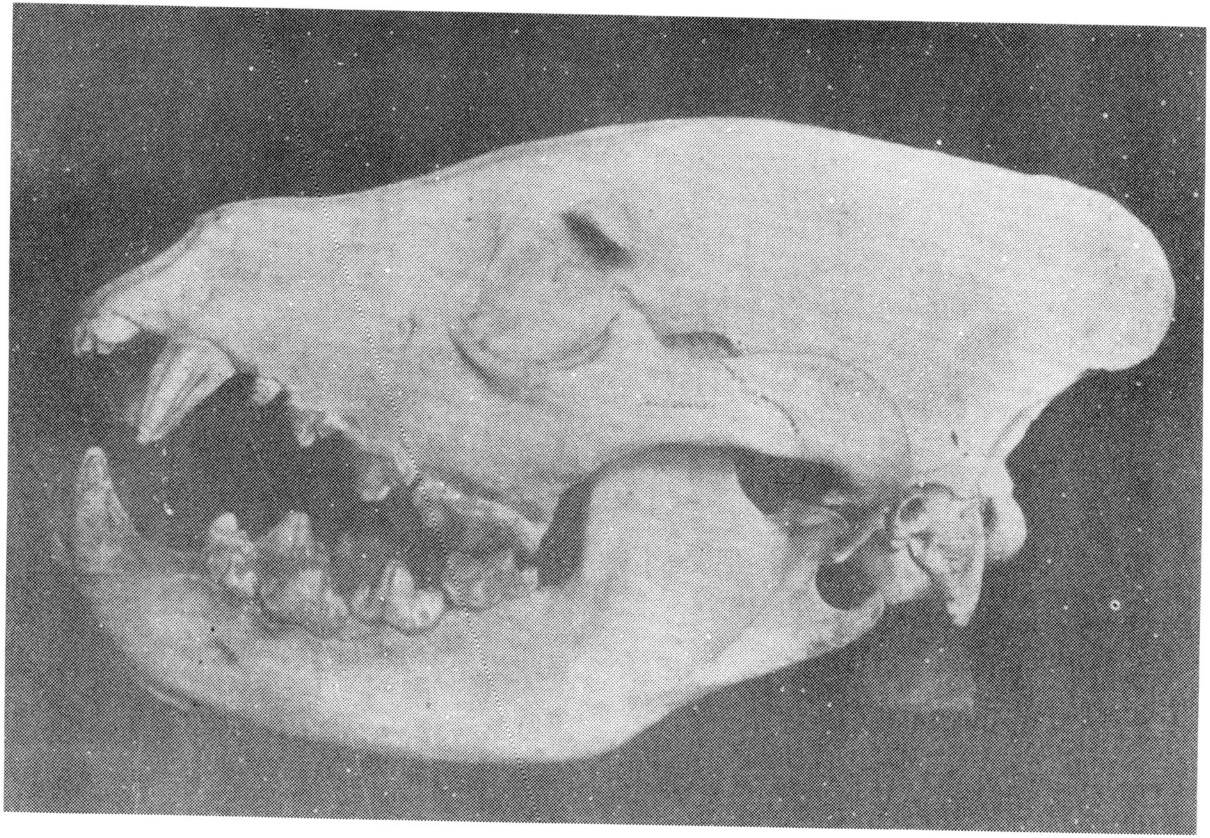

Skull of the Striped Hyaena (*Hyaena hyaena* Linn.).

Few Carnivores have jaws and teeth which can compare in strength and bone crushing power with those of hyaenas.

1

Fig. 1.—Left forefoot of the Large Civet (*Viverra zibetha*).

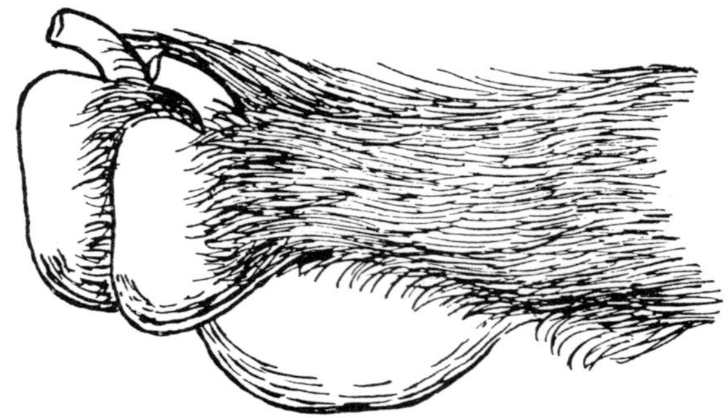

2

Fig. 2.—Right hindfoot of Common Hyaena (*Hyaena hyaena*).

Note the shape and vertical plane of the toe-pads which are uptilted in the Hyaena's foot; the general character of its foot is dog-like and distinct as such from the feet of Cats and Civets.

 Photo by F. W. Champion.

The Striped Hyaena (*Hyaena hyaena* Linn).